THE FAITH OF MODERNISM

THE
FAITH OF MODERNISM

BY

SHAILER MATHEWS

AMS PRESS
NEW YORK

Reprinted from the edition of 1924, New York
First AMS EDITION published 1969
Manufactured in the United States of America

Library of Congress Catalog Card Number: 71-108117
SBN: 404-04266-X

AMS PRESS, INC.
New York, N.Y. 10003

CONTENTS

THE FAITH OF MODERNISM

THE FAITH
OF MODERNISM

CHAPTER I.

IS CHRISTIANITY OUTGROWN?

THE world is being reconstructed. Can Christians aid?

A religion that cannot meet the creative needs of men and women is a social encumbrance. A faith on the defensive is confessedly senile. Æsthetic appeal, vested wealth, the inertia of organization may serve to hide its decadence, but they cannot renew its youth. True, such a religion may serve as a form of social control, like bread and the circus keeping an uneasy proletariat from revolt. So it was in Rome when the rich restored the shrines of the Olympian gods. So it was in France when Napoleon purveyed religion as a hope of heaven to a nation he refused political liberty. So in our world there are those who would make the church only a means of quieting unrest. But such hopes are already vain.

1

The proletariat like the rest of the world refuses
to be quiet. A religion that cannot meet the deepest
longings of restless hearts, that fears freedom of
speech, that distrusts social reconstruction, that
makes respectability its morality, that would muzzle
scientific inquiry will be ignored by a world that
has outgrown it.

I.

Religions spring from human needs. Each has
grown as its teachings and institutions have satisfied creative souls. Each has become an enemy
of progress when it has fastened upon society the
authority of the past. The ideals of the past have
then become the source of injustice for the present;
the hopes of the past, the conventions of the present;
the spiritual achievements of the past, the inhibitions
of the present.

The history of Christianity is one of successive
applications of a religious inheritance to new needs.
Jewish Christianity fulfilled the hopes of the Jews;
patristic Christianity gave metaphysical satisfaction to those who wished for immortality; Roman
Christianity gave order and unity to the Western
world; Protestantism satisfied the needs of those
souls that had been touched by the new spirit of
nationalism and economic independence. Each advance broke the mortmain of the past and led to
reformation. Adventurous spirits like Origen, Augustine, Thomas Aquinas, Luther, Calvin, and Wes-

ley represented the creative needs of their days. The older forms, it is true, have continued, more or less to the advantage of their own progeny, but Christianity has been a creative rather than a restraining power whenever it has satisfied the needs of those who were making to-morrow. Christians have never had a static system of philosophy or a finished theology. They have been moved by a spiritual loyalty to a succession of institutions and groups. These, like a coral island, have been built up by innumerable lives. According to their best intelligence and in response to actual currents of life men have organized methods for expressing their loyalty to Jesus as Savior, and their faith in a loving God. The demand for theological change has not sprung merely from theologians. New human needs, new phases of civilization have demanded satisfaction. Every age has had its Modernist movement when Christian life, needing new spiritual support, has outgrown some element of ecclesiastical coercion and incarnated some new freedom of the spirit. Society has grown irreligious where Christians have opposed religious progress. Social inertia has bred religious decline.

Our own age has grown creative. What the rise of the Roman Empire was to the ancient world, the rise of nations to Western Europe, the rise of democracy to Protestant Europe and America, is the rise of our new social mind seeking new knowledge of reality, liberty, and justice in all social relations, to the present. But to-day, as in the past, creative spirits when asking religious teachers for bread have too often been told to feed on the crusts of yesterday. And there are thousands of men and women who wonder why custodians of the faith should so fear the future that they must elevate the past.

Such questions cannot be quieted by mere pietism or theological dogmatism. The masses are asserting their human worth; economic processes are more complex and are becoming better fitted to personal ends; women are sharing in the privileges of men; education is being democratized; science is reinterpreting and discovering realities; thought is adventurous; religion is being separated from political control; duties are supplementing rights; new nations are gaining self-determination; internationalism is beginning to discover the need of morality; social evils are being converted or destroyed; a new world of freedom is struggling to be born. How shall Christian people maintain their religion as a vital and inspiring force in such new conditions?

II.

But he is a near-sighted optimist who regards social change as always social progress. Its threat of injury is as loud as its promise of happiness. We have not yet learned how to use our new power, our new wealth, our new knowledge, our new ideals, our new freedom. The dangers of progress are as real as the dangers of reaction. The new world is not yet a brotherhood.

Everywhere we find the survival of the psychology of war. For a generation men were taught to suspect and hate nations other than their own. They applied their best intelligence to the organization of armies and navies with which they sought to conquer and control not only backward nations, but their rivals in the struggle for the coal and iron and oil and gold and alluvial land and trade and treasures of weaker folk. When war came upon a world filled with distrust and hatred, treating generosity as hypocrisy or sentimentality, cynical as to human nature, it left men as it found them, still distrustful of each other, still endeavoring to maintain peace by diplomatic intrigue, secret treaties, and military force. A generation trained to hate has continued to trust hatred. It is little wonder we look upon the future with apprehension. Where there should be mutual faith there is suspicion, where there should be confidence there is fear, where there should be hope there is cynicism, where there should be coöperation there are rivalry and intrigue.

Distrusting the future, men seek to enjoy the present. Nations with millions of their children starving abound in those who are feasting. Distrust of spiritual values has given rise to pagan enjoyment of animal life. Contempt of old inheritances has thrown too many men and women back upon primitive instincts. Morality is flouted by thousands in the name of freedom, and in many a community the family has become a temporary mating— if indeed men and women in revolt against the pact and its ideals trouble themselves with marriage. Love is too often but a synonym for animal passion. Men would rather be pagans than Puritans.

Economic development which has proceeded with ever accelerating rapidity for a hundred years has intensified that class struggle which is as old as humanity. Here too is hatred. Those who own machines and those who work machines are grouping themselves in sinister opposing camps, each waiting for some sign of weakness in the other, in order to coerce the other. The increase of wealth has brought increase in discontent. The individual is threatened with submersion in social groups. The Battle Hymn of the Republic is repeatedly silenced by the Marseillaise of the masses.

And because men are desperate, they have grown cynical. They distrust human nature and its worth. The deep motives of life are diseased. The war to end war has bred wars. The treaty that promised peace has given coercion. The idealism of social prophets has been scorned and caricatured by men who distrust and hate their fellows. The cry for justice has too often been silenced by suspicion and abuse. The naturalism of some men of science only makes for deeper distrust of mankind.

Let us be thankful that such dangers are only the darker side of social change; that throughout the world there are voices calling men to repentance and to God; that as never before, there are men denouncing war as criminal, brotherly souls who are seeking to give justice rather than fight for their rights, scientists who are showing God's ways of action, citizens who believe that a better social order comes by self-control rather than by surrender to sensuous enjoyment. But the new world in the making is not at peace.

III.

What have we to meet these needs, born not of intellectual doubt but of social change and human passion ?

Some look to democracy. But as we better understand the democracy of the past and observe its operations in the present, this faith is tempered by apprehension. Will democracy unfold anew the moral quality of human nature ? Will it grade up or grade down human life ? A social order without authorities, subject to the will of the people must rely upon good will and expert knowledge or terror. Not a few observers of society say that the worst enemies of democracy are democrats themselves.

There are those who tell us that material and social forces will adjust themselves as men come to be more intelligent. Science, they say, is a new religion and as men come to see the facts of nature they will also come to wisdom. There is hope in this conviction.

Science is making over social life. Its going forth is like that of the sun and there is no hiding from the heat thereof. Not only in laboratory and study, but in counting house and factories, we find

the conviction that it is is possible to organize creative forces so as to increase their effectiveness. There
is a way of conducting all affairs in accordance with
the facts. Men analyze business as they practice
chemistry. To think of science as a merely academic
matter is to forget advertising and meat-packing,
oil-finding and automobile-building, radio concerts
and a million other things in which the human
mind has grown accustomed to think in terms of
facts and inferences rather than of authority. The
scientific mind is not infallible, for it is lhuman,
but it is suspicious of whatever fears investigation.
For it there can be no God behind a veil too sacred
to be touched.

But when has knowledge meant virtue? After
we have learned how to control nature and have
fully gained social equality and freedom shall we
have learned how to live happily and justly? Knowledge is certainly not always identical with good
will, however much good will must be directed by
knowledge. At bottom every crisis is a matter of
folks.

Nor is our need any less individual than in former
days. Our age of freedom and of power is in danger
of becoming an age of revolt. The eighteenth century
saw revolutions turn special privileges into popular
rights. In our day still other rights have been
gained by the masses, but the question of authority
is still unanswered. If men and women are to be
equals, where is control to lie? Is there to be any
control? How can free persons live together? For

the first time in history there are being formed
a morality and a social order where no man is
recognized as having inherited right to claim su-
periority. Is this to mean moral license and political anarchy? Is any sort of authority compatible
with equality and freedom?

Our new knowledge of natural forces has given
men new power to produce wealth. Economic efficiency is advancing almost geometrically, new
methods of communication are all but abolishing
space and time. Our new chemistry and physics
promise still greater control of material forces in
the future. It is a fearful thing for a civilization
to be possessed of such power. Who can assure us
that it will be wisely used? What hope is there of
any protection against its being used for purposes
of destruction? Is humanity good enough to have
such power?

The answer is tragic: humanity is not good enough.
It must be transformed, regenerated. But if democracy and science alone are not sufficient where is
the power for such a change? We confidently reply,
in Christianity. But can Christianity meet these
needs and change human life? That is the supreme
question of the hour.

IV.

There are Christians who declare it cannot. They
affirm the world can grow only worse instead of
better. Progress is denied and evils alone are af-

firmed. Men and women must be rescued from the world by accepting theological beliefs.

And what are these beliefs? And how are they to be applied?

The world needs new control of nature and society and is told that the Bible is verbally inerrant.

It needs a means of composing class strife, and is told to believe in the substitutionary atonement.

It needs a spirit of love and justice and is told that love without orthodoxy will not save from hell.

It needs international peace and sees the champions of peace incapable of fellowship even at the table of their Lord.

It needs to find God in the processes of nature and is told that he who believes in evolution cannot believe in God.

It needs faith in the divine presence in human affairs and is told it must accept the virgin birth of Jesus Christ.

It needs hope for a better world order and is told to await the speedy return of Jesus Christ from heaven to destroy sinners, cleanse the world by fire, and establish an ideal society composed of those whose bodies have been raised from the sea and earth.

Will such answers to-day bring in the reign of justice and love? Their proponents tell us they do not expect it. Social pessimism is preached as the background of individual hope. The truths that will save men will not save the world.

It is not strange, therefore, that theological orthodoxy no longer appeals to thousands of men and women. It is not heralded as a regenerating power in the modern world. Even granting it true, it will not work such a result. The doctrines alleged to be its fundamentals have been earnestly and even fanatically enforced by the church for hundreds of years, and never more so than in Russia, the Balkan States, Austria, Italy, Spain and France. The results speak for themselves. The appalling fact is that dogmatic Christianity has succeeded in demonstrating its own contention that it has no message for the world's new needs.

V.

Has Christianity then no promise of hope for a suffering world? Can Christianity do no more than its dogmatists?

The history of the Christian centuries, let us be thankful, permits of no such doubt. The Christian movement is far more extensive than its orthodoxies. It has always been a leaven of social righteousness. Theology is autocratic, but Christian loyalty is creative. One has only to read the sermons of the church or watch its social influence to feel the Christian dynamic within and above the creeds. It is no accident that theological change is the work of pastors. For Christianity even when most relying on the civil power has always been more than its theologies. The Christian community has supplied a spiritual influence lifting men gradually from their sins and giving them new ideals. Orthodox Christians are now working for the world's transformation. But the striking fact is that in so doing they are not stressing theological fundamentals. They do not deny them but they ignore them as moral and social motives. And their instinct is wise. The religion of the church is more lasting than its formulas. Four centuries ago, when theology furnished the very battle cries of Christian zeal, it was the Christianity of human hearts that, passing beyond theological logic, and organizing new group-loyalties and ideals, laid the foundations for so much of our modern world.

The Christianity to which the world has always appealed is more than a system of doctrines. *It is a moral and spiritual movement, born of the experience of God known through Jesus Christ as Savior. It is a community of life, not a system of philosophy or theology.*

The insistence that theological doctrines be regarded as the supreme test of Christianity comes from men of the passing generation. To their appeal the youth of the world is increasingly indifferent. *The men and women who are endeavoring to remake our world need moral dynamic.* They have outgrown the theology of earlier days. Like the world-view, the politics and the social customs they embody and represent, our inherited theological tests no longer are recognized by a world in the making. That world is already organizing its religious convictions to meet the new and complicated needs born of new social forces and situations.

No, Christianity has not passed away. Christians are once more finding new power in their religion. An untheological, practical, scientific age is shaping a religious and moral Christianity which has its own intellectual expression and method, its own uplift and revelation; a religion which is as intellectually tenable as it is spiritually inspiring. For Christianity is only the abstract term for the beliefs and practices of Christians. Missionaries are building hospitals and founding schools. Churches are building parish-houses and becoming community centers. Christian Associations are equipping gymnasiums and establishing hotels. Vice is being outlawed. War is being denounced. Social service is broadcasting Christian love. Economic justice is being promised. Denominations are seeking to coöperate in service to men irrespective of race or attainment. Scientists are rediscovering God and statesmen are pleading for the Christian spirit.

Such efforts are new forms in which to-day's spiritual experience of God is finding expression. Is it any less Christlike than He who went about doing good, healing the sick, feeding the multitudes, urging good will rather than coercion, revealing God as Father and men as brothers? The true watch-word of Christianity is not truth, but faith vitalized by love.

Men will always make doctrines to express their faith, but they will give only indifferent assent to those which they do not organize as they seek to meet their imperative needs. Creative minds care less for their father's beliefs than for a faith that respects their increased knowledge and stimulates their will to serve. A theology that must be enforced is a religious Blue Law.

To meet the world's questions and needs frankly, to substitute persuasion for coercion, to honor freedom of thought, to trust the power of truth, to make our Christian inheritance an individual and social dynamic, to help it do for the creative forces and the evils of our age what the men of the past made it do for their ages—that is the task of Modernists. Not to deny but to affirm; not to doubt but to act; not only to call Jesus Lord but to keep his commandments; not to arouse new theological controversy, but to show that the Gospel of Jesus is at one with other ways of God's workings; not to dispossess men of their theological inheritance, but to help them to express that inheritance in effective forms of modern thought and institutions; not to substitute sociology for God but to coöperate with God in our social order; not to deny that individuals need the saving love of God, but to show that love can be more trusted and better expressed because of the new knowledge given us by science—these are the hopes of Modernists. And inspiring their hopes and helping in their tasks is their unfaltering trust in Jesus Christ as the revealer of God's way of human salvation.

CHAPTER II.

MODERNISM is a projection of the Christian movement into modern conditions. It proceeds within the religious limits set by an ongoing Christian group; it distinguishes permanent Christian convictions from their doctrinal expression; it uses these convictions in meeting the actual needs of our modern world.

The term Modernism itself is somewhat unfortunate. Despite all protestation to the contrary it gives the impression of self-satisfaction, as if only those who hold certain views are intellectually abreast of the times. Yet the terms "Modernism" and "Modernists" have come into such common use that they cannot be avoided. This much, at least, can be said in their favor: they indicate a real tendency in our religious life. This tendency is to be seen when one compares the intellectual habits of Christians as they expound Christianity. Some rely on scientific method; others, on church authority. The former may be said in general to be those indicated when Modernists are mentioned. But strictly speaking, "Modernism" and "Modernist" imply no

15

new theology or organized denominational movement. The habits of mind and tendencies of thought which the terms have come loosely to represent are to be found in all Christian groups in all parts of the world. Until Modernism is distinguished from fundamentally theological interests, it will be misunderstood. Modernists are not members of a group which prescribes doctrinal views, but Christians who use certain methods of thought are described as Modernists. These methods, with their points of view, must be considered in detail.

I.

There are two social minds at work in our world. The one seeks to reassert the past; the other seeks by new methods to gain efficiency. Such attitudes are the result of our human nature. In all life there are inheritance and variations. All human affairs have their "youth movement" and their "stand patters." Between the two there is always more or less of a struggle. We see it to-day in literature, art, business, and international politics. It is, therefore, only natural that they should appear in the field of Christianity.

Christianity is not a hard and fast system of philosophy or orthodoxy accepted by all those who call themselves Christians. It is that religion which Christians believe and practice. There have always been differences within the church and these differences have been of many sorts. But at bottom

Christianity has been the attempt of men to rely upon Christian principles in meeting the needs of their actual life-situations. In making such attempts two types of Christians have always been found. There have been those who, without serious recognition of moral imperatives, have wished to enforce inherited beliefs and institutions; and those who have sought to examine their inheritance, reject whatever has been outgrown and restate its permanent elements from the point of view of and for the satisfaction of new needs. Social and cultural changes, due to forces of many sorts, have lain back of such theological readjustments.

This was the case when non-Jews came to replace Jews in the early church; when the barbarians inundated Western Europe; when economic and political changes brought about what we call the Reformation; and later when churches were founded in America. Indeed illustrations are all but innumerable of the tendency of life in changed social, economic, intellectual conditions to bring about readjustment and even revolution in vital Christianity. Just because the present is so abounding in change it is to be expected that persons in sympathy with forces that are making to-morrow should follow the practice of the past and carry their new and, in their opinion, better modes of thought and living into their religion. Such persons naturally, and properly, have been called Modernists.

Over against them stand those who either do not clearly see the needs of the world, who are not in

sympathy with the reconstructive forces of to-day,
or who have not yet used them to make religion
more effective. Such persons are committed to the
religious formulas and methods of the past and find
in the past the authority for religiously meeting present needs.

But one fact must be recognized. The differences
between these two types of Christians are not so much
religious as due to different degrees of sympathy
with the social and cultural forces of the day. For
lack of better terms we may distinguish them as
Confessional or Dogmatic and Modernist Christians.
Neither term is derogatory or precise. One group
emphasizes heredity and the other variation. The
one grounds truth in an appeal to authority, the
other on inductive methods. Both are professedly
loyal to Christ, but the Dogmatist makes the Bible
rather than Christ basal. Both are endeavoring to
apply the Christian religion. Each is satisfied with
its respective positions. Yet it is plain that the views
of neither satisfy those who are in sympathy with
the other social mind. It is therefore, for the sake
of mutual understanding and in no spirit of controversy that the Dogmatic or Confessional and the
Modernist or scientific views of Christianity should
be compared.

II.

Let us start, then, with this obvious fact: the issue
between Modernism and Confessionalism is not one

of mere theology. It is rather a struggle between two types of mind, two attitudes toward culture, and, in consequence, two conceptions as to how Christianity can help us live. The Modernist and the Dogmatist are not debating on quite the same plane; one is interested in theological regularity; the other with religious development and scientific method.

The two parties belong to no single religious group. The Roman Catholic Church was, in fact, the first to feel the sharpness of the struggle between them. Abbé Loisy, Father Tyrrell, not to mention other distinguished Roman Catholic scholars, attempted to apply scientific methods to the study of the Bible in the interests of increasing the prestige and power of the Roman Church. Pius X condemned the movement in the famous *Encyclical* "Pascendi Dominici Gregis" of 1907. The *Encyclical* refers to Modernists as men "lacking solid safeguards of philosophy and theology, nay more, thoroughly imbued with the poisonous doctrines taught by the enemies of the Church and lost to all sense of modesty." They are said to "lay the axe not to the branches and shoots but to the very root, that is, to the faith in its deepest fibers." "They play the double part of rationalist and Catholic . . . and there is no conclusion of any kind from which they shrink or which they do not thrust forward with pertinacity and assurance." "Relying upon a false conscience they attempt to ascribe to a love of truth that which is in reality a result of pride and obstinacy." The *Encyclical* goes on to declare that the Modernists are agnostics, believers in religious immanence (by which is meant that religion springs from the impulse to satisfy need), a view which would lead them to consider all religion as both natural and supernatural.

The presentation of Modernism as a philosophy and a denial of Christianity is a part of a widespread polemic. As such the charge by Pius X—and with less consistency by the Protestant dogmatists—is good controversial strategy, but it is not correct. It is merely a method of controversy which is as old as humanity. Its technique is briefly this: group your adversaries together into a party; give that party a name; give that name a bad meaning by attaching to it your own interpretation of its champions; and then attack opponents without discrimination as representing the evils which have been attributed to the name.

The representatives of Modernism in the Roman Church have strongly and acutely opposed this strategy and in their reply have set forth in considerable detail their own idea of method and procedure. Instead of an attempt to "degrade the person of the divine Redeemer to the condition of a simple and ordinary man," they point out that their method is first of all a painstaking examination of the historical elements of the New Testament, including the relationship of the thought of the New Testament Christians to their times; that Modernism so far from being as the *Encyclical* says: "a synthesis of all heresies," is simply an attempt to assist the church to meet the crises set by modern philosophy, science, and social organization. Thus they seek to make plain that the issue is between Christianity identified with its scholastic and dogmatic interpretation and Christianity as a religion whose tenets and doctrines are subject to historical development.

The position of Protestant dogmatists is to all intents and purposes the same as that of Pius X. All over the world they are asking ministers and teachers to answer "Yes" or "No" to questionnaires concerning belief in the literal inerrancy of the Scripture; the deity and virgin birth of Jesus; the substitutionary atonement offered by Christ to God; the biblical miracles; the physical resurrection, the ascension, and the physical return of Jesus from heaven. The acceptance of all these supernatural elements, they hold, is essential to real Christianity; they are the "fundamentals" without which religion is not Christianity.

This opposition to the Modernist interpretation of Christianity is not born of mere belligerency or unthinking reaction. In the minds of many earnest Christians it expresses a genuine desire to maintain orthodox Christianity as a vital religion, and a fear lest Modernists should be substituting sociology or scholarship or even unbelief for the Gospel. And with this fear a Modernist must confess sympathy. A religion that psychologizes God into a personification of social values, that belittles sin and the need of salvation through the working of God's Spirit, that would merely substitute a liberal theology for a conservative, is impotent to help a bewildered and sinful world toward the Kingdom of God. But a man is not a Modernist because he disbelieves orthodox theology. Modernism is hardly less different from Confessionalism than it is from Unitarianism. Both Confessionalism and Unitarianism are on the same plane of theological rationalism. Modernism is concerned with the historical method of discovering the permanent values of Christianity, and the religious rather than the theological test of religion. It is not aiming at a system of theology but at organizing life on a Christian basis. It can be understood only as one frankly admits that the Modernist is deliberately undertaking to adjust Christianity to modern needs by changing the emphasis in its message and by historically evaluating and restating the permanent significance of evangelical Christianity to human life. If Christianity is essentially only what the seventeenth century thought it, a theological system inherited from the past, the charge that Modernism is un-Christian is logically sound. But it is just such a concession that the Modernist would rather die than make.

III.

What then is Modernism? A heresy? An infidelity? A denial of truth? A new religion? So its eccesiastical opponents have called it. But it is none of these. To describe it is like describing that

science which has made our modern intellectual world
so creative. It is not a denomination or a theology.
*It is the use of the methods of modern science to
find, state and use the permanent and central values
of inherited orthodoxy in meeting the needs of a
modern world.* The needs themselves point the way
to formulas. Modernists endeavor to reach beliefs
and their application in the same way that chemists
or historians reach and apply their conclusions. They
do not vote in conventions and do not enforce beliefs
by discipline. Modernism has no Confession. Its
theological affirmations are the formulation of results
of investigation both of human needs and the Christian religion. The Dogmatist starts with doctrines,
the Modernist with the religion that gave rise to doctrines. The Dogmatist relies on conformity through
group authority; the Modernist, upon inductive
method and action in accord with group loyalty.

An examination of the Modernist movement will
disclose distinct aspects of these characteristics.

1. The Modernist movement is a phase of the
scientific struggle for freedom in thought and belief.

The dogmatic mind found its natural and most
effective expression in the Roman Catholic Church
and in the Protestantism of the sixteenth and seventeenth centuries. Because it developed under the
influences of Roman law, its possessors were trained
in the methods of the lawyer and the schoolman, and
dominated by deductive logic. It regarded doctrine
as of the nature of law and church-membership as
an obedience to theological statutes passed by church

authorities. Its range of interest in philosophy was practically limited to Aristotle, and its theological method was to organize texts of the Bible and bring about the adoption of the resulting formulas or dogmas as authoritative statements comparable with a legal code. Protestantism preserved most of these dogmas while setting up new authority for accepting them. It was not interested in the church as an historical movement, but in the literature of the first stages of that movement. It detached the Bible from history and declared it to be the sole and divinely given basis of revealed truth. Yet the Bible it accepted was determined by authority, and biblical truth was authoritatively said to be expressed in creeds and catechisms and Confessions adopted and enforced by authority. The dogmatic mind has always sought to express its beliefs sharply and clearly and with condemnatory clauses. Its century-long anathematizing of heretics shows that it is quite as truly interested in keeping non-conformists out of the church as in expressing truth held by the church. Naturally it has never been primarily interested in science, international peace, or social justice. It has often attacked scientists; it has never thought of abolishing war; and it has preferred charity and heaven to economic readjustment. One of its most bitter controversies has been over the relation of "works" to faith.

We must in justice distinguish between the dogmatic mind relying upon authority and Christians who approve of dogma. One has only to read the biographies and the histories of the sixteenth and seventeenth centuries to see how many Christians responded to deeply religious and social motives and rose superior to the intensely theological atmosphere in which they lived. Such men were Melancthon, Thomas Moore and Grotius—many of whom suffered persecution. The persons who wrote the Confessions of the sixteenth and seventeenth centuries, which are now said to be final, were the same people who made themselves secure by executing, imprisoning, or banishing their opponents and confiscating their property. It was they who carried on the Wars of Religion in France, the Thirty Years' War in Germany, the Civil War in England, and the wars between the Spaniards and Dutch in Holland. Loyalty to a church was identical with loyalty to a nation. To break with dogma was like a break with a law. In the nature of the case, if Christianity as thus conceived is the only Christianity, the treatment of dogmas as law will continue.

Theological controversy has seldom if ever tended toward Christian love. If one party won, the other party lost. The winner disciplined the loser. Whether Roman Catholic or Protestant, Calvinist or Arminian, the ecclesiastic has never insisted that salvation involved the acceptance of some formulas essentially moral. Neither the Apostles', the Nicene, the Chalcedonian, nor the Athanasian creed makes any reference to morality beyond the mere statement of the belief in the forgiveness of sin. So far as each is concerned, the teaching of Jesus contained

in the Sermon on the Mount might as well never
have existed. The same is not equally true of the
great Protestant Confessions, but the chief interest
in all those Confessions is theological rather than
ethical. According to them faith is not merely an
attitude of loyalty to Christ, trust in God and an
application of truth to life, but an acceptance of some
doctrinal formula.

This is not to say that the church has been indifferent to morality. Any such assertion would be
scandalously untrue, but the "fundamentals" of salvation have not been seen by the dogmatic mind in
the field of morals or religious experience but in
that of authoritative theology. To hold heretical
doctrine was to be assured of hell fire; not to believe
in some theological tenet was and still is in the
minds of some Christians to make entrance of
Heaven impossible. The dogmatic mind has never
been as severe with sinners as it has been with
heretics.

Such a position is easily understood. Dogmas and
confessions like oaths of loyalty and constitutions
make easy tests. It was natural that conviction of
the finality of such tests should become permanent
in groups which originated in theological controversy
and which were either prosecuted, or persecuted, or
both. Confessions adopted for political as well as
religious purposes are still used as a test. That is to
say, the habit of making dogmas a test of Christianity is a survival of an age when men looked
upon Christianity as identical with its doctrines and

upon its doctrines as law and upon coercion as warranted by the danger of heresy.

But Christianity is more than dogma. It is and always has been a way of ordering life and its institutions. The insufficiency of dogmatic Christianity to express fully the religion of Jesus Christ has always been felt. Especially of late since the days of Moody, evangelical Christianity has been developing a layman's theology which has placed increased emphasis on practical religion, the love of God and His readiness to receive those who seek Him. Thus many doctrines once judged invaluable for Christian living have been tacitly outgrown. It would, for instance, perplex the majority of Presbyterians to give the Five Points of Calvinism, yet three hundred years ago these were vehemently asserted and enforced by the Reformed churches. One might go on indefinitely showing how doctrines are not repudiated, but cease to function in the life of earnest Christians whose attention has shifted from technical theology to practical religious interests.

The simple fact is that the center of interest in religion is passing from theology to life. This tendency is bound to demand intellectual justification other than inherited authority can give. Men seek to answer questions of practical living suggested to their religious faith by methods successful in other fields of inquiry.

There are thousands of persons both within and without the churches who distrust the ability of the dogmatic mind to meet such questions. To them the conception of Christianity as a legal system is untenable. They will not be coerced into religious conformity. They demand freedom in belief. They prefer no theology to what seems to them an irrational and ineffective theology. It is these men and women threatened by new temptations, possessed of new powers, new knowledge, new discontent, facing new problems and new tasks, determined upon intellectual freedom, whom the Modernist would serve. The Dogmatists may, if they can, serve others.

The habits of medieval Catholicism and national churches, the appeal to some supernaturally authoritative church or Bible, arguments based neither upon a study of the nature and history of either Bible or church, but upon usage or ecclesiastical action, do not satisfy free minds. There is an indubitable struggle between ecclesiastical authority and free scientific method. The two have never been compatible. The Modernist, conscious of his loyalty to Jesus Christ, recognizes the value of all theologies, but with him scientific method has replaced the philosophy and the patterns with which the church fathers defended and organized Christian truth as well as the church authority with which their formulas have been enforced. He, too, has propositions for which he would die, but the freedom he asks for himself he would grant to his opponents. If he had the power to enforce his own beliefs on the church he would not use it. Truth can be trusted to find its own defense in efficiency.

The new movement in evangelical Christianity is, therefore, not to be understood by emphasizing its points of difference with systems of theology. It can be appreciated only as one recognizes that it is the outcome and expression of the Christian life of those who rely upon the inductive method as a way to reality and upon freedom as imperative in religious thought.

IV.

2. Modernists are Christians who accept the results of scientific research as data with which to think religiously.

It would, of course, be unsafe to accept every scientific theory as material for theological thinking. But the Modernist starts with the assumption that scientists know more about nature and man than did the theologians who drew up the Creeds and Confessions. He is open-minded in regard to scientific discovery. Believing that all facts, whether they be those of religious experience or those of the laboratory, can fit into the general scheme of things, he welcomes new facts as rapidly as they can be discovered.

When, therefore, he finds experts in all fields of scientific investigation accepting the general principle of evolution, he makes it a part of his intellectual apparatus. He does this not because he has a theology to be supported, but because he accepts modern science. He has no illusions as to the finality of this or that theory, which, like Darwinism, attempts, though imperfectly, to describe an evolutionary process, but he is convinced that scientists have discovered that there is continuity of development in the physical world, and that, therefore, such continuity must be recognized by religious thinkers. He is cautious about appropriating philosophies, but he is frankly and hopefully an evolutionist because of facts furnished by experts. In this attitude he is reproducing that of earlier religious thinkers when they abandoned the Ptolemaic system of the universe and adopted the Copernican. When he wants to estimate the worth of dogmatic hostility to such attitudes he recalls the attack upon the views of Copernicus by those who had identified Ptolemaic science with religion, and waits for good people to show good sense.

Furthermore, in the light of sociological and historical facts, the Modernist uses the methods of science in his quest for religious assurance. He knows that the Christian religion develops as a group-possession when men's experience and knowledge grow. He is not content simply to accept a doctrine. He seeks to understand its real purpose and service. He therefore seeks to discover why it arose. He searches for its origins and estimates its efficiency in the light of its conformity with social forces and its capacity to nerve men and women for more courageous living. The beliefs of Christians are less extensive than the loyalties of Christians. A religion is a way of living and the Modernist refuses to think of it as an accumulation of decrees. Attitudes and convictions, he discovers from a study of the Christian movement, are not identical with the language and concepts in which they are expressed.

3. Modernists are Christians who adopt the methods of historical and literary science in the study of the Bible and religion.

From some points of view, this, although not the most fundamental, is their most obvious characteristic. It was the critical study of the Scriptures with which the movement started in the Roman Catholic Church and it has laid the foundation for theological discussion in Protestantism. The Modernist is a critic and an historian before he is a theologian. His interest in method precedes his interest in results. The details of his attitude as to the Bible will appear in a later chapter, but in general the Modernist may be said to be first of all a Christian who implicitly trusts the historical method of an approach to Christian truth.

Modernists believe themselves true to the spirit and purpose of Jesus Christ when they emphasize his teachings and the inner faith of a century-long movement rather than the formulas in which aspects of this faith were authoritatively expressed. In this Modernists are doing for Christianity what Americans did for Americanism when they changed their Constitution in order to give truer application to the principles the Constitution itself expressed. Men who abolished slavery and gave the suffrage to women were more consistently expressing the principle of

liberty than the framers of the Constitution themselves, for they limited suffrage to men and permitted
the existence of slavery.

4. The Modernist Christian believes the Christian
religion will help men meet social as well as individual needs.

Any acquaintance with social facts makes plain
how responsive the individual is to social influences. Any intelligent religious program must take
such facts into account. But programs differ. Some
emphasize rescue and others emphasize salvation.
The dogmatic mind has always preferred rescue. In
practice it has varied from the asceticism of the
monk to the rejection of social idealism. In theology
it has limited salvation to elect individuals. On the
other hand, students of society know that the relation of the individual to the social order involves
him in responsibility for social actions as well as
liability to social influences. Therefore, they undertake to transform social forces for the benefit of the
individual. Such a policy is furthest possible from
a belief that humanity needs only better physical
conditions. It is a solemn affirmation that the Christian cannot hold himself guiltless if he permits the
existence of economic, political and recreational
evils, and that he will be the victim of such evils
if he does not undertake to correct or destroy them.

Modernists believe that the Gospel is as significant
for social forces as for individuals. They find little
hope in rescue of brands from burning; they want
to put out the fire. They believe that the same

God who so loved the world as to give his only begotten Son that those individuals who believe in him might not perish, also sent his Son into the world that the world might be saved.

But when the Modernist speaks of saving society he does not believe that society will save itself. He believes that the constant need of God's gracious help is to be understood as clearly through the laws given him by the sociologist as by the psychologist. He, therefore, hopefully undertakes to apply the Golden Rule to group-action as truly as to individuals. He would carry Christian attitudes and convictions into our entire life. He urges the duty of sacrifice on the part of nations and of classes, whether they be employers or employees, as truly as on that of individuals. For Jesus Christ to him is more than the savior of isolated individuals. He is the savior of men in society.

This is one reason why the Modernist is an object of suspicion. The dogmatic mind is almost always to be found among social reactionaries. To no small degree Modernism in theology is opposed because Modernists urge reform in economic matters. In the struggle over economic privilege the Modernist is properly feared as one who takes Jesus seriously and believes implicitly that his Gospel applies to wages and war as truly as to oaths, charity and respectability.

5. The Modernist is a Christian who believes that the spiritual and moral needs of the world can be met because he is intellectually convinced that Chris-

tian attitudes and faiths are consistent with other realities.

In so far as by trustworthy methods he reaches intellectual conclusions not in accord with those reached by deduction or by major premises given by authority, the Modernist knows himself an emancipator. Christianity is under suspicion in so far as it refuses to submit any tenet to impartial scrutiny. Each intellectual epoch has made that scrutiny. Modernism as a scientific method is for to-day what scholasticism and legal methods were to the past. It is no more negative than is chemistry. If all its conclusions are not the same as those previously held, it is because some things are established beyond question and the perspective of the importance of beliefs has been determined. A scientific method cannot start with authority because it cannot assume conclusions at the beginning of its investigation.

6. Modernists as a class are evangelical Christians. That is, they accept Jesus Christ as the revelation of a Savior God.

The Modernist movement is, therefore, not identical with Liberalism. With all due respect for the influence of Liberalism in clarifying religious thought, its origin and interest tend toward the emphasis of intellectual belief and the criticism and repudiation of doctrines *per se*. The Modernist like any other investigator has a presumption in favor of the reality of that which he is studying. Both historically and by preference his religious starting

point is the inherited orthodoxy of a continuing
community of Christians. To this group he belongs.
The place of evangelical Christianity in social and
ethical life, the aid it gives to millions of human
hearts, the moral impetus it has given social reforms, forbid treating Christianity as an unborn child
of human thought. But if it is to carry conviction
as a way of organizing life it must be studied and
applied according to methods judged effective by
those to whom it is recommended. As the early
church fathers were Christians who utilized their
Hellenistic training to expound the Christianity
brought them by Jews; as the Schoolmen were Christians who followed Aristotle; so the Modernists are
Christians who use scientific method to estimate
and apply the values of that evangelical inheritance
in which they share. One might as well expect a
student of politics to deny the existence of the State
as to expect a Modernist to be disloyal to the Christian church; to expect a student of medicine to be
indifferent to human ills and skeptical as to the
use of medicine, as to expect that investigators within
the Christian church should be indifferent or skeptical as to faith.

In brief, then, *the use of scientific, historical, social method in understanding and applying evangelical Christianity to the needs of living persons, is
Modernism.* Its interests are not those of theological
controversy or appeal to authority. They do not involve the rejection of the supernatural when rightly
defined. Modernists believe that they can discover

the ideals and directions needed for Christian living by the application of critical and historical methods to the study of the Bible; that they can discover by similar methods the permanent attitudes and convictions of Christians constituting a continuous and developing group; and that these permanent elements will help and inspire the intelligent and sympathetic organization of life under modern conditions. Modernists are thus evangelical Christians who use modern methods to meet modern needs. Confessionalism is the evangelicalism of the dogmatic mind. Modernism is the evangelicalism of the scientific mind.

CHAPTER III.

DEEP within the Modernist movement is a method of appreciating and using the Bible. This is inevitable. Even the most superficial observer knows that the Bible is the basis upon which much of our religion has been built. But how shall men accustomed to scientific methods of thought use it for religious ends? Need they use it at all? They would be foolish not to. In using it, shall they give up their scientific attitude? That is impossible. Shall they treat the Bible merely as one of the ethnic literatures? That would be of incalculable injury to the religious life.

The true method is followed by the Modernist: to study the Bible with full respect for its sanctity but with equal respect for the student's intellectual integrity. We must begin with the facts concerning it, interpret its actual value and use it for what it is actually worth. Only thus can it properly minister to our spiritual needs.

I.

The Modernist, when he appeals to biblical teachings, wants, first of all, to find the facts concerning the Bible.

For nearly a century the Bible has been studied scientifically. Such study has not started from the assumption of supernatural revelation, but has sought information regarding the origin, time of writing, and the integrity of the biblical material. No one doubts the legitimacy of such attempts. They do not spring from theological bias; they do not deny doctrine; they simply seek to obtain information. They are those used by all students of literature and history and are no more anti-religious than a text-book in chemistry is anti-chemical. But no sooner do men thus study the Bible than facts appear which make belief in its verbal inerrancy untenable. As facts they naturally must be accounted for. In consequence there has grown up a general view of the Bible which is basis of the Modernist position. It was never voted upon or formally adopted by any group of scholars. Like views commonly held in biology or any other science, it is the result of investigators working without collusion, sometimes in rivalry, but without dogmatic assumptions, seeking to find and organize facts by scientific methods. Now that their work in the critical field is largely done, we find general agreement as to how the Bible originated, how it was composed, where it was written, why it was written. Differences as to details exist but the world of undogmatic biblical scholarship is certainly as much at one as to these matters as are the various theologies. How complete is the result of this study can be seen from the fact that there is no serious attempt to refute its conclusions by its own methods. There is plenty of anti-critical literature, plenty of denunciation of higher critics as enemies of the faith, plenty of attempts to enforce conformity in views of doctrines declared to be the teaching of the Bible; but there is little appeal to method and facts. It could not be otherwise. One cannot use the methods of critical scholarship without adopting them. Once adopted they can be trusted to give trustworthy results.

At the present time, although men may differ in their theology, in the extent to which they follow their methods, and in the frankness with which they give utterance to their views, there is no recognized biblical investigator who does not use the methods of criticism when studying the Bible to obtain knowledge of its origin, time of writing and composition, or who does not accept the general theory of the structure of the Pentateuch and synoptic gospels. Even so conservative a theologian as A. H. Strong declares "we may concede the substantial correctness" of the Pentateuchal analysis, and limits inspiration to religious ends.

II.

By their historical and critical study men have found that the Bible is composed of literature gradually gathered in the course of centuries. But, in fact, if one wished to be academically accurate one should speak of Bibles rather than a Bible. The Hebrew Old Testament is composed of three col-

lections.   To these collections were added in the
Septuagint or Greek Old Testament, another, The
Apocrypha, containing eleven more writings.   Thus
the Jews had two sacred collections, the Hebrew and
the Septuagint.   There does not seem to have been
any hesitancy in using the Greek translation of the
Hebrew Old Testament, but the eleven extra books
of the Greek Old Testament were not regarded as
possessing the same authority as the others.

The writers of the New Testament used both of
these Old Testaments.   Many of the quotations of
the New Testament are from the Septuagint.

When the Christian movement started it had no
New Testament and its first literature seems to have
consisted in letters written by Paul to some church
on issues suggested by the new faith in Jesus.   There
were also various collections of sayings and anecdotes
concerning Jesus circulating among the churches,
some of which came from the apostles.   Gradually
these collections coalesced and took permanent literary form in different parts of the Roman Empire.
Christian literature, however, by the second century
was considerable, and there arose the question as to
which of the writings that were circulating among
the churches were trustworthy and authoritative.   It
took centuries for final answers to be given the question, and even then the answers were not identical.
By the middle of the second century the churches
seem to have agreed that the collections of biographical material which we now know as the four Gospels were from the apostles, and that there were

thirteen Pauline Epistles, an apostolic Book of
Acts, an Epistle of Peter and another of John. Beyond this there was a wide difference of opinion and
no final agreement. Most of the great churches except those of the West rejected the book of Revelation.   Some churches wished to include in their
New Testament other writings such as First Clement,
Barnabas, the Gospel of the Hebrews and the Shep-
herd of Hermas.   Thus it came to pass that there
were different canons for the New Testament approved by various churches, none of which was that
adopted by the Roman Catholic church and now
held by Protestants. A final decision as to these
books was reached in the Roman church at the Third
Council of Carthage in 397, but the same church at
the Council of Trent added to the collection those
so called Apocrypha which were in the Greek Old
Testament.   Thus we have at the present time the
Bibles of the Roman Catholic church, of the Protestant churches, of the Armenian church, of the Coptic
church, and of the Syrian church.   *There is no
single Bible accepted universally by Christians.*
The test of admission of a book to the canon was
simple. Out from a large number of writings which
circulated among Christians of the second century
as the works of Peter, James, Barnabas and other
contemporaries of Jesus, the churches gradually
selected those which they regarded as authentic. The
test was, therefore, in essence, critical.

The dogmatic mind rests content with giving authority to this grouping. But such passivity is im-

possible for one who would test the trustworthiness
of this decision of Christians who lived hundreds of
years after the books were written, and almost as
many years after the original manuscripts had disappeared. He, as well as the Christians of the fourth
century, would seek to discover the real contribution
of ;the Bible to his faith, and therefore he seeks to
discover the authorship and the time of writing of
the biblical literature.

Nor is such investigation fruitless. Practically
the same general results have been reached by independent scholars. True, details of their findings
vary, but there is practical unanimity in the belief
that the Pentateuch and many other Old Testament
writings are combinations of much older material;
that the biblical material has been subjected to
successive editings; that many of the Old Testament
writings are centuries younger than the events they
record; and that several of the New Testament books
did not spring from apostolic sources in the sense that
they were written by the apostles themselves.

These results of the study of facts are a starting
point for any real understanding of the Scriptures,
and should be a common-place among all ministers
and church members. The object of such study is
not "to cut the Book to pieces" but to arrange it
chronologically. At the end of thirty years of widespread critical and historical study of the Scriptures
it would seem as if ministers, at least, would know
these conclusions. The fact that the rank and file
of ministers are not only unacquainted with a scien-

tific study of the Bible, but are ignorant of some of the more elementary facts concerning the Scriptures is a commentary on the working of the dogmatic mind.

III.

The Modernist believes in studying the Bible according to accredited historical and literary methods. These methods, though not theological but scientific, are used in the interest of the religious life.

One does not need to be learned in order to see that biblical literature often expresses religious truth in ways that are not literal. We instinctively feel that expressions attributing to God face, hands, hair, back and kidneys are figurative. Few persons assert the legitimacy of interpreting such expressions literally. But what limits are to be set this concession? If the Bible is to be taken as verbally inerrant, then we must hold that God has hands large enough to cover the cleft in the rock in which a prophet hides. Not to take it literally is to abandon the principle of inerrancy formulated as a doctrine. That opens up the whole question as to the proper method of interpretation of all the biblical situations. It is this method which the Modernist endeavors to shape and use. His aim is to do intelligently and methodically throughout the entire Bible what the average Bible student does instinctively or allegorically in certain passages. When his work is done he has an intelligent view of the development of the biblical literature. By its use he can see the growing faith in God and, what is far more important, the growing revelation of God's character through the prophets and Jesus Christ. No one, of course, will claim that any method is beyond the range of human frailty. Historians and critics are men of like passions with the theologians. The ultimate question is whether we have the right to use responsible literary methods in interpreting the Bible as a record of the growing knowledge of God sufficient, when properly understood, to be regulative in our own lives. To such a question the Modernist unhesitatingly replies that he has such a method and that it gives facts upon which a helpful use of the Bible can be based.

The value of such a conclusion has been questioned on the ground that if the Bible is not historically and literally accurate at one point it cannot be trusted at others. Such an opinion evidences the dogmatic type of mind, but it cannot be respected by those who seek to know the facts. The Bible has always been seen to contain material of different value for the spiritual life. From the days of the allegorists of Alexandria to our own day, Christians have adopted other than literal interpretations of the Bible, although most of these ingenious methods have been abandoned as artificial and untrustworthy. The Modernist having adopted a method approved in all similar studies, *finds in the Bible the product and the record of a religion;* and this religion he not only traces through the biblical period, but can project into his own day and the day of his children.

For his method enables him to distinguish trustworthy from questionable beliefs of an ancient civilization recorded in a literature.

IV.

The Modernist studies the Bible to discover the characteristics of his religion and to share in the faith of its founders.

The understanding of the literary nature of the Bible as well as of the literary methods of the contemporaries of Biblical writers determine the Modernist's treatment of the Bible material. He knows that its literary forms and methods are those of the time of writing. When, therefore, he finds that among the literary habits of the time is the use of symbols, of rewritten history, of folk-tales, he is prepared to examine the biblical material impartially and without apprehension. Whatever may have been the estimate of such literary forms on the part of those to whom they were immediately addressed, there is no doubt that they express a genuinely religious attitude. A study of the pre-Christian and Jewish literary methods results in the discovery of what this attitude and this ultimate purpose were. If it should appear that certain stories of the Bible were legend rather than sober history, this would simply mean that the past expressed its religious attitude and conviction by the use of legend. Similarly in the case of pictures of the future which characterized the preaching of the early church. Certainly they are no more literal when found in the New Testament than when found in the non-biblical pre-Christian writings of Judaism with which recent studies have made us so familiar.

And so throughout the entire Bible. Having discovered the time of authorship and the type of literature of a biblical book it is easy to determine the way in which it is to be used. To say that this is a denial of the Bible is, of course, easy. It is urged that if one portion of the Bible is folk-tale and so cannot be given full historical weight, we cannot be sure that all of the Bible is not of the same sort. The answer is simple: The dogmatic mind cannot be sure. It does not recognize or correctly use the facts of the Bible.

But there are methods by which we can tell whether the Bible is history or not. Such methods require intellectual attention and training as truly as any other scientific procedure. The inability of the uninstructed to understand Christianity has always been asserted by dogmatic authority. What the Modernist is doing is, therefore, nothing new. The Christian church in its study of the Scriptures has never delivered itself into the hands of the un-intelligent leader. The work of men like Clement of Alexandria, Chrysostum, Ambrose, Augustine, Bernard, Francis, Thomas Aquinas, the Schoolmen, Luther, Melancthon, Calvin and Wesley, that is to say, of the very men who have shaped Western Christianity, makes it plain that their treatment of the Scriptures is no farther from that of the believer in literal inerrancy than from that of the Modern-

ist's. They all insisted that revelation must con-
form to realities of the universe and in their interpretation they took pains to show that such agreement
existed with the universe as they knew it. If ordinary grammatical interpretation left them in any
uncertainty, they promptly found an allegorical
meaning in the Scriptures which satisfied the demands of what they regarded as truth. The Modernist rather than the champion of verbal inerrancy is
a true successor of such fathers of orthodoxy. His
regard for the Bible is just as sincere, his use of
the Bible for building up the spiritual life is no
farther removed from an assumption of inerrancy,
his attempt to understand the experiences of God in
the Bible are no less intellectual than theirs. And
he knows how to separate between the permanent and
the temporary in its pages.

The real issue in the case of the Bible is deeper
than the question as to whether it is inerrantly inspired. What we are really concerned to gain is a
conception of the Christian salvation.

The Bible when properly arranged on the basis
of satisfactory evidence is a trustworthy record of
human experience of God. In point of literary character and method it is just what might have been
expected from our knowledge of the literary habits of
the periods in which its component parts were
written. Thus annals, history, laws, poetry, folk-
tales, preaching, although incomparably superior in
content, are of the same literary class as the contemporary literature in so far as it has been recovered.

By a comparison of such facts the Modernist is able to use the Bible as furnishing trustworthy material for the discovery of what its writers thought or recorded others as thinking.

The mere fact, however, that a belief has been recorded in the Bible accurately does not guarantee its permanency or accuracy. That must wait upon other than literary tests. A legitimate distinction can therefore be drawn between the words of the Bible and the teaching of the Bible. The latter is to be found in the experience recorded in the Scriptures properly estimated in its historical surrounding.

It is well to reassert this difference as the heart of the Modernist's position regarding the Bible. It is not negative but positive. He does not deny the truth of the Scriptures. On the contrary, he is devoted to the Scriptures and the endeavor to place them in their true position in modern life. Many of the most spiritually helpful studies in the field of biblical study are from Modernists. The difference between the Modernist and the dogmatic theologian does not lie in degrees of loyalty to or respect for the Bible, but in *the method of using it and the presuppositions with which it is studied*. Confessional theology uses the Scripture as itself supernaturally given. The Modernist uses Scripture as the trustworthy record and product of a developing religion. Here again he is at one with many so-called conservative theologians who explicitly say that the writings of inspired men are the record of a progressive revelation and not the revelation itself. *Through the Bible, as through all historical documents, the historian gets to the actual current of human experience, attitudes, convictions.* By such study he is enabled not only to describe what this experience was, but also to discern the tendency of the historical process shown in the succession of institutions, hopes, and beliefs of the religion of which the Bible is the record.

This distinction between a literature which is final in itself and a literature which is a door through which one enters the earlier stages of the Christian religion, is of great help to one who seeks God in human experience. It opens the way for using the fullest intellectual equipment in understanding not only the Bible but the total religious movement of which the student himself is a part. There grows upon one a new conviction of the worth of that religion the origin and the earlier stages of which the Bible records. Through the critical and historical study of the Bible the Christian scholar finds himself the heir of those men of faith whose lives he has come to understand. Christianity becomes not the acceptance of a literature but a reproduction of attitudes and faith, a fellowship with those ancient men of imperfect morals whose hearts found God, whose lives were strengthened by the divine spirit, whose words point out the way of life, and who determined the inner character of the Christian religion. From such sources the major doctrines of Christians are derived. Other elements are secondary accretions from contemporary religions, easily and repeatedly separated from the religion of Jesus Christ.

It is difficult to make this plain to those who know nothing of the scientific use of documents. True, as Protestants, they distinguish between the major and secondary elements of the theology they inherited from the Roman Catholic church, but to them any statement in the Scriptures is material to be used for the construction of any theological edifice. To the Modernist any statement of Scriptures is to be located in its proper historical environment and seen as the expression of the religious attitude of men in that environment. The Bible sprang from our religion, not our religion from the Bible.

The unity of the Christian revelation is found in the unity of a growing religion. In discovering this experience of God and accepting it as his own religious ancestry the Modernist affirms the trustworthiness of the Scripture. He is forced by the discovery and estimate of facts to be loyal to the spirit of the biblical religion. It is this concrete religion which, like all progenitors, has set the sharp limits within which Christianity has developed. The Bible is, therefore, of incalculable value to a modern Christian. He draws inspiration from its pages. But since the religion of biblical characters is distinct from the Bible its product and record, in reproducing as best we can the faith of prophets and apostles, the spirit of Jesus and the loyalty of the early disciples to Jesus, we are not burdened with the impossible task of proving that the Bible is an infallible text-book in all fields of human knowledge. It is a trustworthy record of a developing experience of God which nourishes our own faith. It is all the more trustworthy because it makes plain that God was experienced and His will taught through a variety of social institutions, scientific beliefs, ethical ideals and the literary methods, each dependent upon contemporary culture.

There is no static religion or standardized formula in the Bible. In that fact is one of the most significant of the Modernist points of view, *viz.,* that the true attitude toward God and the true experience of his presence are possible and discernible in the midst of imperfect and even mistaken scientific and other views. The author of Genesis may declare that the sun and stars were created after the creation of the earth and plant life, a conception which our knowledge of astronomy shows is incorrect. But this error does not prevent our sharing in the author's faith that in the shaping of the universe, God was present. So, too, it is only something to be expected when we find in the religious experiences of men who lived before the siege of Troy conceptions of God which to our Christian morality seem unworthy. Such conceptions are, however, no bar to the discovery that with all the human infirmities attributed to Him, the Jahweh of the Book of Judges possessed qualities which had only to be expanded as men's experience expanded, to give the righteous monotheism of the prophets. Belief in the providence of

God can be expressed in poetry, folk-tale and legend just as truly as in literal statement.

In consequence, the Modernist enjoys the spiritual ministry of the Bible quite undisturbed by objections which the believer in the inerrancy of the scriptures has either to answer or to denounce. Poetical statements as to the sun standing still, the story of Jonah, miracles like those of Elijah and Elisha and some of those of the New Testament, can be used at their full religious value. Whether they are sober history or not they are current ways of expressing belief in God's care for men. They are material for understanding the developing consciousness of God and a growing religion. They were contemporary ways of expressing religious faith. In them the Bible is recording trust in a good God whose law is righteous and whose love and power are coextensive. From such a trust we gain help as we seek to have a kindred faith in our day. We face our different tasks and problems in accordance with their trust in God. Our knowledge has grown, but we are still "sons of the faithful Abraham."

Thus, although the historical and critical study of the scriptures does not begin with a doctrine of inspiration, Modernists believe in inspiration rather than inerrancy. But in the inspiration of men, not of words. Men were inspired because they inspire. In this Modernists are one with writers of the Bible themselves, for inspiration within the Bible is always regarded as the experience of the Spirit of God on the part of some individual.

With confidence, therefore, and with the enthusiasm of those who intelligently open up a treasury of religious inspiration and moral guidance, we approach the Bible. We read it not only for its spiritual appeal; we honor it, so to speak, as the germplasm of a developing religion. We seek to discover in it information regarding the origin, development and nature of the Christian faith in order that attitudes and convictions which grew with its characters' growing understanding of God and found fullest and effective expression in Jesus Christ and inspired the religious group he founded, may be more influential in our own lives and in our modern world. We search the Scriptures that we may have life and find them testifying to him whose words are spirit and life.

CHAPTER IV.

As by proper historical and literary methods the Modernist has come to a trustworthy understanding of the Bible, so he also undertakes to analyze and evaluate historically the Christianity which he has inherited. For Christianity is more than "the religion of a book." It is the religious movement that continues the religion recorded in a book. As the Bible is the product and record of the first stages of the Christian religion, so the Christian religion carries forward a progressive religious experience. Into its development have gone the hopes and spiritual adventure, the prayers and faith of millions. To profess it is to feel its romance as well as its truths. It is a sword cast into human history. Men are its champions or its enemies. It cannot be discussed dispassionately. It means everything or nothing. To understand it is to distinguish between its permanent and temporary elements. To gain this understanding we must study more than the Bible. We must trace the long line of human lives which have formed the community of Christians. On the basis of such study Modernists distinguish between doc-

54

trines and those permanent convictions of the Christian religion in accordance with which they would order life.

I.

The community of men and women who have developed our religion is older than its theology. Its earliest records are to be studied in the Scriptures. And what intensity, of hope and fear, of tragedy and joy were theirs! Evidently they did not merely preserve their primitive convictions and institutions. Warrior and prophet, nomad and farmer, sinner and saint, formed their lives into that current of religious experience that set from simple Semitic practices to the worship of the Temple and the preaching of men on whose lips was the fire of God's Spirit. One attitude, however, was in control of that development: the loyalty of the Hebrews to Jahweh as their sole God. It was no abstract faith. From Jahweh they received laws, in His name the prophets spoke, in His service was the way to national prosperity, and in His help lay hope for national greatness. This loyalty was constantly tested by circumstance. Again and again the pressure of foreign nations suggested the abandonment of Jahweh, but just as often there arose some strong soul who showed how faith in its God could enable the nation to meet its crisis. Even sufferings and defeat were within His purpose. By this expansion of the thought of Jahweh required by national growth and trials the religion itself grew.

Hebrew faith was not vagrant. The religion of the prophets is the religion of the ancient Hebrews enriched and matured by constant readjustment to the needs and ideas of many centuries. The elaborate ritual of the Herodian temple was the child of the sacrifice of the desert. The noble words of the prophets were new expositions of Jahweh's power and love and righteousness.

But the Hebrew religion did not develop uniformly. It was not merely a ritual. It was no philosophy of the lecture hall. There were always those whose hearts were exceptionally aflame with the hope that Jahweh was to give the nation the control of the world. The group which expected Him to send some one empowered by His Spirit to accomplish this end was much in evidence in the time of Jesus. While not neglecting the sacrifices of the Temple they awaited the fulfillment of the promise of the coming of a divinely established Jewish kingdom. Sometimes by attempted revolt, sometimes by circulating apocalypses—a code literature of revolution—these persons were building up a group within the Jewish people. These were those who awaited the Messiah.

It is from this group of Jews preserving and embodying not only the faith of the ancient Hebrew religion but also the expectation of a coming kingdom, that the movement of Jesus drew its followers. They clung to the Hebrew religion, but despite all odds they attached their Messianic hope to Jesus. He was the One whom God had empowered by His own resident spirit to be the savior of his people. Christianity in its inception was the religion of a group of Jews who added a burning faith in Jesus as Christ to their religious inheritance. The New Testament shows plainly the bitterness of the struggle between the inherited and new elements of Judaism. Apparently the enemies of the new faith were victorious. Jesus was executed. But the victory served only to consolidate the group formed by his followers. The Christian community grew conscious of its unity and its mission. It held to God's promise of salvation.

But again changes in beliefs came as the membership of the group changed. Others than Jews joined it. It was inevitable that the question should arise as to whether loyalty to Jesus as Christ involved full acceptance of the Jewish religion of the original group. The answer was simplicity itself: those who accepted Jesus as Christ, the revealer of God's salvation, did not need to become Jews. But this new group from which gradually the Jews disappeared, did not abandon all elements of Judaism involved in their new faith. Ethnic continuity was replaced by religious continuity. The new group took over certain elements of the Old Testament religion as a part of its inheritance. It did not take over the Jewish ritual, but it did take over the monotheism and the prophecies of the Jewish religion. The Old Testament became a book of oracles and laws giving direction and support to the new movement. Thus the Christian group continued the deepest convictions of the religion of the ancient people. De-

spite the fact that Jews ceased to be numbered among
its members, the church trusted in God's power to
save.   For had not the Christ appeared?   But there
is no break between the New Testament Christians
and their successors.   The movement is continuous.
Individuals died but the group continued.   It is in
the religious attitudes and convictions of this group
as it developed through the centuries its central faith
in Jesus as the revealer of the saving God that we
discover the permanent elements of Christianity.

II.

If we are to understand our religion we must, therefore, do more than study its formulas and institutions.   We must look beneath and through the Creeds
and Confessions to the attitudes and convictions, the
needs, temptations and trials, the prayer and rites,
in a word, the actual religious life of the ongoing
and developing Christian group.   We must discover
when a doctrine arose, for what purpose it was organized, what religious attitude it expressed, what
unifying social practice or idea it used as a "pattern."
From such a study the conclusion will be clear that
while formulas are a part of our religion they are
not to be identified with that religion.   They spring
from the effort of Christians in different situations
to organize their lives and carry their daily burdens,
perform their varying tasks, not only with prayer and
sacrifice but in loyalty to the inherited attitudes and

convictions of their group regarding God and Jesus Christ.

Nor is this all. A study of the origin and purpose of our doctrines shows how patterns have originated and served actual needs of a group. By them attitudes and convictions are given expression in doctrines. But they are not of necessity the same. Convictions are individual; doctrines are social. Convictions inspire attitudes; doctrines are "accepted." Convictions are to be expressed dramatically as well as intellectually; doctrines are analogies and social patterns raised by common usage and group authority into symbols of convictions. Through a knowledge of their origin and a sympathetic interpretation of patterns used in doctrines we discover the basal attitudes and convictions they express. And these are more fundamental than their expression.

Such facts are by no means limited to religious development. In the evolution of democracy and of our Christian religion alike, human experience, human need, human hopes, human weaknesses, working within a group readapt its social inheritance to new situations. There is variation as well as the heritage of common traits. No one would mistake a democratic social order for an imperialistic. Both seek to maintain order; both may do many things alike; they may have identical habits and institutions; but each follows a different line of reproduction and growth according to inner tendencies. Just as political convictions express themselves in laws intended to meet varying social needs does the in-

herited inner control keep the Christian movement
to the reproduction of distinct types of group life and
ideals.

Indeed one may press the analogy further. The
English constitution is not a written document, but
the immanent tendencies of English life always free
to meet new conditions with the same purpose and
control. But at certain crises, when threatened by
a policy or ambition hostile to this inner control, the
English people have adopted some definite formula
which like Magna Charta, the Act of Supremacy, the
Act of Settlement, the Bill of Rights and the Habeas
Corpus Act, have assured the permanence of the general development. They are experience codified as
social control.

Similarly the Christian community in its struggle
with the problems of sex and property and war
has repeatedly organized doctrines to assure the permanence of its convictions. Such specific formulas
have kept the activities and beliefs of the Christian
group from straying into unsafe fields because they
have effectively expressed its inner and persistent
convictions. The development of new doctrinal patterns was not philosophical but, like the documents
of the English constitution, the outgrowth of the inability to meet new needs and tasks with inherited
convictions expressed in inherited patterns. Each
attempt failed because the older terms and concepts
were ineffective media. But the very effort to fit the
attitude and the convictions of the Christian movement to new situations suggested new patterns. One

after another they have emerged from the actual situations. Sacrifice, ransom, honor, satisfaction, Messiah, "persons," King, law, disobedience, punishment,—these are but a few of the patterns used by men striving to make the Christian view of God and salvation a source of inspiration and guidance in facing life's problems and tasks.

III.

The first duty of the student of Christianity is to seize firmly the historical fact that it is the *concrete religious life of a continuous, ongoing group rather than the various doctrines in which that life found expression.* Now a group is not held together by merely rational elements. Long after any such bonds of union, if they ever existed, have vanished, a group is held together by the assimilation of new members who carry on its practices and cherish loyalty to it as a group. This is one reason why theology is not a philosophy. Its very history shows that it is an organized group belief, born of social forces, ministering to needs socially felt, conditioned by social habits, and using social and other patterns to express its fundamental and determining convictions.

It is easy, if not common, to regard theology as a philosophy of religion. Many theological teachers say the approach to Christian truth is through philosophy; that one cannot have a system of theology unless he has a thoroughly sound philosophical foundation.   Undeniably the importance of philosophy in the history of Christianity is considerable, for Aristotle and Plato have each been the guardian of Christian orthodoxy.   But when one asks not what theology might be or ought to be, but what it actually is, it is clear enough that it is very different from a philosophy.   Contrast, for example, the Presbyterian, or any other formulated theology, with Platonism, or any other so-called "school" of philosophy.   Certain differences at once appear.   There never was a Platonist General Assembly which adopted a Platonist Confession.   Theology as distinct from individual opinion is the organization of a group belief formed as Christians react to the needs of concrete situations.

Recall the course of events which led to the organizing of various theologies.   Without exception, they presuppose conscious needs and are the result of imitation, customs, discussion, conflict, compromise, and successive decisions in groups who claimed to represent the religion of Jesus and endeavored to make it effective in their lives.   They appeared only gradually as a phase of social life.   Christianity began when those believing Jesus was the Christ formed the first group of Christians, and expressed their individual attitudes in group action.   This group multiplied itself in other groups of believers, which though small rapidly joined and expressed their common beliefs in councils or assemblies or something similar.   The theology, for example, of most Protestant bodies gathers around some Confession which has been adopted by some church body, representing a group of groups. In fact, most Protestant theology historically is the organization of the theological beliefs of various states and cities. The very names of the Confessions preserve their origin.

These facts are so generally recognized both by the Catholic churches and by historians that one needs only to be reminded of them to see that the mass of creeds and affirmations which constitute theology is the accumulation of decisions of innumerable groups of men. A diagram of the descent of Protestantism would ultimately lose itself in the innumerable local and provincial councils of the Roman Empire.

Further, these various decisions have usually been enforced by group-authority as well as by argument. Variety of individual opinions has always existed but church groups seek self-preservation by compelling individuals to assent to decisions which express fundamental convictions. In ages when liberty was unknown, Christian trust in God was too precious to be left to private misuse. Excommunication from the church and punishment by civil authorities both alike were summoned to give success to orthodoxy or the official beliefs of a group. Historically speaking orthodoxy is, therefore, the product of a strange pedigree. The executioner and the persecutor, the jailer and the torturer, the politician and the intriguing woman, as well as saints, scholars, and martyrs, have contributed to the growth of that enforced consensus of belief which made a theology a standardized group belief. Whatever might have happened if circumstances had been different, the historical fact is that the decisions of successive councils, Greek, Lutheran, Calvinist, Anglican, Presbyterian, in fact of every ecclesiastical body able to get control of the machinery of the state, owe their success over the views of opposing groups or individuals to group-authority. Men felt eternity was at stake, and there was no place or time for self-deception. Loyalty to the church included loyalty to its authoritative doctrines.

It was inevitable, therefore, that those doctrines became permanent which were held by the political and social groups which were dominant. Heresy is the belief of a defeated party. If it had succeeded it would have been orthodoxy. A striking illustration of this fact is the history of the Nicæn formula during the reigns of various Roman emperors. Arian and Athanasian doctrines were successively authoritative. But those groups who held the Athanasian views finally got control of the state and the church, and their beliefs became accepted as essential to the Christian life. The success of the later bodies which gave permanent organization to Christian teaching always lay with those who could enforce their decisions. From the exclusively historical point of view, the issue between groups holding opposing views was not so much one of truth as of ability to enforce a decision. The decisions reached by the fathers of orthodoxy were usually nearer the truth than the views proposed by heretics, but their survival was due to vital social forces rather than academic discussion. They satisfied the religious needs of an evolving social order.

The social origin and consequent efficiency of doctrines is also seen in the fact that many of them are the outcome of religious customs and practices maintained by groups as aids to primary Christian loyalty. They were a secondary or apparatus-Christianity. Thus arose the doctrines of the mass, baptismal regeneration, transubstantiation, the veneration of relics, the worship of Mary, the calling upon saints, the use of images, the infallibility of the Pope speaking *ex cathedra*. None of these doctrines springs from the religion of the biblical characters. Customs grew up, became characteristic of groups and then of larger groups, until they became so common, significant, ancient and sacred as to be elements in the Christian religion itself. Loyalty to the group made it impossible to remove them except by revolution. Rather than face such a crisis Christian groups have explained them, made them into doctrines, and enforced them with authority. Indeed, one of the chief differences between various Christian groups, notably between Roman Catholics and Protestants, is precisely in those doctrines which originated in, preserve and systematize religious practices, most of which were derived from the pagan world. This secondary Christianity is easily distinguished from the primary Christianity that continued the religion of the Bible.

IV.

All our inherited doctrines were begotten in human struggles for something nobler than men possessed. Latin and Protestant theology is composed of the doctrines which were held by the very persons who made our modern world. Orthodoxy may be described as the doctrinal system which sprang from and satisfied the needs of the creative groups who developed Western civilization. That civilization and Western theology have the same line of ancestry.

The social psychology of the one is the social psychology of the other. The patterns of each are alike. Both, as the product of the stronger rather than the weaker group life, reproduce those social forces that met and overcame the difficulties which beset progress.

The process recorded in the New Testament continued as the years passed and the Christian group began to express its common faith in Christ under different social conditions than those of Palestine. The major doctrines of Christianity have been not so much thought out as lived out. The community of the faithful found themselves exposed to crises which their fathers either had not known or had not faced. They were forced to consider, not only the truth of their religious inheritance, but also its capacity to help them live under new conditions. They wanted to live more in harmony with their God and their times. The men and women who constituted the century-long Christian movement have been struggling with intellectual and social tasks forced upon them by the conditions in which they lived. Speaking broadly, each great doctrine emerged from a particular social epoch and took form in some pattern which preserves a particular habit of life or dominant social interest of that period. It is this fact that enables us to understand why there should be such variations in the development of the Christian religion as appears in the Coptic, Nestorian, Armenian, Greek, Roman and the innumerable Protestant bodies. Each is the possession of some group holding to Jesus as the revelation of the divine will, but subject to different geographic, political, economic as well as ecclesiastical influences reflected in the history of human life. The civilization in which there has been no development has never had a developing church. But a developing church has meant doctrinal instability.

Western civilization has not been peaceful. It has developed in a series of crises, sometimes tragical. The collapse of the Western Empire, the change in social practices because of a vast immigration, the slow reëmergence of orderly social life through feudalism, the economic and cultural changes of the Middle Ages, the rise of nationalities and the decline of feudalism, the revolutions which marked the rise of capital; all these have forwarded Western civilization. Each set up conditions of life in which Christians shared. Each furnished a characteristic pattern in which a fundamental conviction was expressed as a doctrine. A sketch of the rise of doctrinal patterns will make this plain.

The simple faith of the Jewish Christians that
Christ would establish the kingdom of David led
them to kindly and pious living, but its nationalist
patterns did not fit the needs of the men who were
not Jews and were not interested in Jewish national
hopes. These Gentile men and women who believed
in Jesus as the revealer of a saving God sought to
organize life in accordance with their conviction.
Their religion helped them care for the poor, love
their family, honor charity, endure persecution. But
as children of their own age they did something more.
They began to rationalize their faith. Greek Christians did not much discuss sin or social matters.
Rome did not permit agitation for reform. With
minds nurtured in philosophy and the mystery religions they felt that salvation born of faith in Jesus
as the Savior was due to the transformation of the
human nature by contact with the divine nature. To
this transformation they attributed the resurrection
of the flesh as well as of the spirit. A literal metaphysical contact of divine and human natures in an
incarnate person was, therefore, a matter of vast con-
cern. It was a real demand of minds in search of
reality. In response to this need, and in terms set
by the conditions which gave it rise, there emerged
from centuries of discussion and struggle the Trinity.
In it a philosophical monotheism was expressed in
the terms of biblical religious experience. Such a
doctrine was something more than philosophical affirmation. It was an element of a vital religion, the
test of loyalty to the Christian group itself. Men of

the Greek world felt that any doubt as to the metaphysical identity of the substance of the Father and of the Son not only argued disloyalty to Christ but made their experience of salvation unthinkable. And the central pattern belief of their assurances of salvation through Jesus Christ was drawn from paternity; the Father begot the Son.

When the Christian movement developed in the Western part of the Roman Empire it found itself in the midst of new difficulties. It accepted the metaphysical formulas established in the fourth and fifth centuries, because such doctrines had become a part of their loyalty and were enforced by severe discipline both civil and ecclesiastical, but the disintegration of the Roman Empire and the instinct of the Western world for administration gave rise to new doctrinal tendencies. The Christian group, trained in political rather than speculative habits, facing a world falling to ruins, began to think of men's relations to God in terms of Roman imperialism. New experiences gave new patterns. The Roman Catholic church became in form and genius a transcendentalized Roman Empire. The tri-personal God of metaphysical theology became a supreme monarch issuing decrees, and punishing violators of the laws. Men's sin arose from Adam's disobedience which corrupted human nature itself. Each man propagated sin and corruption in his descendants. All human beings were, therefore, born morally impotent and doomed to hell. God elected certain members of this guilty race to be saved and to be forgiven, but for such gracious act He had no reason but His own sovereign will. The very tragedy of the times argued man's worthlessness and God's supremacy. Pessimism as to the world and desire for salvation made thousands celibate; the monk became the ideal Christian. Men needed strong doctrines to meet the suffering of the hour. And the church survived social chaos because it was made fit to survive by its reliance upon divine grace. From the days when civilization grew desperate before its threatened collapse came our doctrines of original sin and the sovereignty of God, not as speculations of the study but as helps for the conduct of life and as supports of Christian faith in an age of tragedy.

With the immigration of northern peoples into the decadent Empire, the human stuff of European civilization changed. Feudal practices dominated men's minds as the very basis of human relations. Such practices found expression in Anselm's doctrine of the atonement, by which God is conceived of as feudal lord having an honor which must be satisfied before He is free to undertake the salvation of man whom He wished to take the place of the fallen angels. Only in a medieval pattern could the medieval mind see justice in forgiveness and an explanation of "why God became a man."

The rise of nations shaped national churches which, while repudiating Roman ecclesiasticism, perpetuated almost the entire theological scheme of the imperialistic Roman church. Secondary Christianity was all but abandoned, but primary Christianity with its doctrines preserving biblical doctrines continued. But under new political conditions, experiencing the new control of national monarchies, patterns changed. Men conceived of God as a monarch, and of His relations with men as subject to conditions identical with those which were found in the new states. It is no accident that Protestantism has never succeeded within the boundaries of the old Roman Empire. Social inheritances there were too fundamentally imperialistic to yield to individualism.

The *bourgeois* period has given us a modification of Calvinism, the supreme example of the sovereignty pattern, in the interest of the new sense of the rights of man. The theology like the politics of the period sensed freedom and developed the rights of man over against not only kings but God. From democracy with its new independence arose self-determining religious groups like the Congregationalists, Baptists, and Unitarians, which were never state religions like Lutheranism, Anglicanism, and Presbyterianism.

Such facts as these make it impossible to believe that theology is any more static than the world in which its makers lived. The effort to order life and meet its problems in the spirit of loyalty to Jesus Christ has always given rise to new applications of the Christian inheritance. New occasions teach new doctrines. Therefore Christianity is always developing as groups of Christians change in personnel and face new tasks. Theology is the variant legitimatization of constant attitudes and convictions. The method of this legitimatization has been the use of new patterns for belief, usually drawn from the state. Theology since Augustine has been transcendentalized politics.

V.

This sketch of how group convictions of Christians have found expression in social patterns will help us to understand the relation of doctrines to permanent Christian faith:

1. Theology is functional. This appears when we discover why some pattern-doctrine appeared. Beneath it and expressed by it are profound convictions and attitudes which are ever seeking effective expression. Nobody ever sat down like a philosopher to create theology. Even Origen, the first theologian, found a body of beliefs already held by the churches. Each doctrine developed as it was needed by the Christian communities of a certain period. Theological change followed social change. The Christians of each period inherited the beliefs of their predecessors. In so far as this heritage failed to satisfy new needs, they reëxamined it and found in it values which were capable of expansion and restatement as beliefs in new social patterns. Beliefs (or doctrines) are thus to be distinguished from the attitudes and convictions they express.

A theological pattern of unchanging content has never existed. Theological terms imperfectly mirror experience. Their truth is not of the order of mathe-

matics or science, but of law and life. As long as
they are not so regarded, theological agreement is
impossible. Each group reads its own experience
into its formulas be they never so much alike in
terms. From loyalty to the group using such terms,
schisms, sects, and denominations are born. A doctrine, historically considered, is true when in an effective pattern it expresses and legitimatizes the
Christian group's faith in Jesus as Savior. But
such faith is exercised under conditions in which it
lives and by which the total life of a group is affected.
The intellectual content of a doctrine is secondary to
its ability to represent continuous group loyalty. Men
have not been Christians because of doctrines, but
they have drawn up doctrines because they were
Christians—believers in Jesus Christ.

When a pattern no longer expresses a religious
value or serves as the symbol of a group attitude, it
should be and has been abandoned. This is noticeable
in current religious discussions. Confessional theo-
ology perpetuates a vocabulary once representative
but which means little or nothing to much religious
life of to-day. This is one of the causes which have
brought technical theology into disrepute among the
rank and file of Christians. For persons to say that
they are religious but care nothing for theology is
simply a way of saying that they find the terms used
by theologians meaningless. The reason for this is
plain. They no longer intelligibly express any attitude or loyalty judged essential in our social order.
They are outgrown patterns. Yet these same per-

sons will strenuously insist upon the use of certain other terms which are the very battle flags of their inmost convictions. A vital theology uses terms which have accepted meaning as social patterns and symbols. It is idle to force men to use terms which have no such meaning or symbolism.

2. One chief means of identifying terms with group loyalty and so accustoming Christians to the group use of some pattern, has been discussion. By the concentration of group attention upon terms its beliefs become unified. The words grow so accustomed that they signify their group's vital interests. Only thus can terms and symbols have any more than an individual or sectarian meaning. When a term by constant use has come to represent the deepest convictions and attitudes of a group, it is a symbol of such elements. So we can best appreciate the passion with which Christian groups arrayed themselves under such terms as "consubstantial" and "like substance." They were never precisely defined but they evoked and represented actual attitudes and loyalties. And these mattered greatly. The groups using these terms were not merely debating metaphysics. They constituted antagonistic tendencies toward monotheism and polytheism. It meant everything to the development of the Christian movement that the group of strict monotheists under the banner of "consubstantial" finally won. Otherwise Christianity might have been committed to pluralism if not to polytheism. As it was the terms became symbols of attitudes rather than sharply defined concepts.

A discussion to enforce terms which do not express the religious interests of a group serves to deaden religion itself. Discussion of problems of religious education and the application of the Gospel to social affairs is helpful, because the discussion is always aimed at some moral or religious attitude; its terms have immediate relation to religious experience; and formulas help the organization of groups possessing their attitudes. On the other hand, a discussion, let us say for example, over the order of the decrees would to-day have no such meaning, whatever value it may have had in the seventeenth century. Its terms and concepts no longer represent the group loyalties of Christians.

By accustoming Christians through discussion to patterns codifying new applications of Christian attitudes, progress in religion is made possible. True, dogma, or authoritatively defined group belief, changes slowly and with much opposition, but already within the last twenty-five years we have developed by the usage demanded for discussion, a vocabulary which is the functional equivalent of the seventeenth-century vocabulary. It is not composed of words sharply defined but those which have acquired such emotional associations as to represent the dynamic attitudes of the groups using them. While there may never be an absolute consensus of opinion, discussion is certain to emphasize some fundamental conviction symbolized by terms in common usage. Doctrines are thus the means by which a group expresses its inherited convictions. They will continue to develop as long as religious thought is free.

3. Since theology is functional, we can understand why the same Christian attitudes and loyalties have been and still can be expressed at different times among different groups by different patterns and formulas. This is evident in the history of such words as "Christ," "Son of God," "Savior," "Lord." But it is equally true of other terms. *The common divisor of Christian groups is their attitude toward God as revealed in and by Jesus.* The theological patterns in which this has been expressed have repeatedly changed as new social needs give rise to new religious needs.

VI.

This historical study enables us to recognize that the permanent element of our evolving religion resides in attitudes and convictions rather than in doctrines. The process of making theology does not involve the abandonment of values and attitudes which outgrown patterns expressed for their authors, for these are preserved by the continuing group itself. New patterns, however, are found which will more constructively express these loyalties under new conditions. Theology changes as banner-words change, but Christian experience, conviction, attitudes, prayer and faith will continue. For, although group interests and consequently accepted patterns change, Christianity has bred true to itself. It has been developed by a continuous group of Christians whose needs and satisfactions and loyalties have been of the same general type.

In Christianity as in every developing movement both heredity and variation are at work. The word Christian has a meaning that is more specific than "religion," and less specific than "Catholic" or "Protestant," "Baptist" or "Methodist," "Orthodox" or "Modernist"; but its primary content like that of all social movements is not that of definition, but of a group's power to perpetuate itself by reproducing similar institutions, attitudes and beliefs in successive but genetically related groups. In the Christian movement there is progress or decadence, evolution or retrogression, but always within discoverable limits. Herein Christianity illustrates a general law. The original little *eohippus,* for example, set both the limits and the line of development possible for that strain of life which was to produce the modern horse. At first glance there seems to be very little similarity between a Percheron and the little fox-like creature of ancient days, but structurally the modern horse is the same as its ancestor. The line of descent has always been within the limits set by that ancestor. No descendant of *eohippus* was ever bird or worm. As each new species responded to new environment and grew in size and efficiency, it reproduced the structure and dominant qualities of *eohippus.* Similarly in the case of a religious social movement like Christianity. With all its wealth of individual opinion, its history has been within limitations, determined by convictions and attitudes of the original Christian group recorded in the Bible—a development set by what might in biological terms be called its dominant reproductive inheritance. We gain these convictions by considering the natural history of their expression in patterns.

VII.

What are these controlling convictions of the Christian movement which the succession of doctrinal pattern have expressed?

Looking back to the original group which first embodied fundamental Christian attitudes in current social patterns, we find ourselves among the Jewish contemporaries of Jesus Christ himself. Their loyalty to him as the revelation of the saving God is historically primary. In our journey to this group we pass beyond all formal theology, all church organization, the New Testament itself. The Christian movement produced each one of these through the applications of its convictions to its needs. The original disciples of Jesus had no theology. Yet they were Christians. It is impossible to believe that Jesus as founder of a religious movement should have not taught its fundamental values. If we examine the earliest records of his life we find no dogma. He did not demand belief in the inerrant Bible, his virgin birth, his atoning death (in the medieval sense of the term), his physical resurrection, or his physical return. The tests of orthodoxy were not the tests established by Jesus. Such a

statement as this does not necessarily imply that
doctrines are untrue. That is a matter for considera-
tion. But if Christianity is a development—as historically it is—of the original group-loyalty to Jesus
himself and his teaching as to divine forgiveness and
entrance into the kingdom of God, its fundamentals
are not those of the dogmatic mind. Whoever heard
Jesus demand that in order to be saved men should
believe that God was a substance existing in three
hypostases or that he himself possessed one person,
two wills, a human nature consubstantial with humanity and a divine nature consubstantial with the
Father? He may have been all that these statements
mean, but he did not demand that people believe
such propositions, nor were they for centuries regarded as essential elements in Christianity. The
reason why this is not commonly understood is that
organized groups of Christians have not only believed
it possible to draw up statements to meet their own
needs, but they have also undertaken to identify their
doctrinal patterns with Christianity and to enforce
and perpetuate them with the aid of political and
ecclesiastical authority. Thus the true office of doctrines to aid Christians in expressing Christian convictions and attitudes for the satisfaction of vital
needs has been obscured. But nevertheless Christians have always advanced in religious efficiency by
acting in new circumstances in accordance with basal
rather than merely descriptive interests. The Christian movement has always embodied the same attitudes and convictions, because loyalty to them is im-

plied by loyalty to the group. This loyalty has found expression both negatively and positively.

Negatively, loyalty to the Christ has never made men atheists, polytheists or pantheists. The Christian community has never made vice sacred or flattered human nature as sufficient to its needs, or minimized the suffering arising from sin. It has never preached hatred or fatalism or belittled divine forgiveness. It has never denied the need or the fact of God's participation in salvation nor believed that man was without responsibilty and power of repentance. It has never denied immortality nor detached it from morality.

On the other hand the Christian community has embodied in its doctrines the following convictions:

Man needs God's help and salvation if he is to be free from sin and impersonal nature including death.

God, maker of heaven and earth, is fatherly and forgiving; He shares in humanity's sorrows and struggles, and because He loves men is engaged in saving them both individually and socially.

Jesus Christ is the revelation in human experience of God effecting salvation. His life, death, resurrection and words offer the practicable way of fellowship with and consequent aid from God, as well as ideals for human conduct.

Good will, though never fully realized, is of the nature of God, and is the law of progress, the foundation upon which human society can safely be built, the only moral motive which reproduces in human life the spirit of God and the example of Jesus.

Individual human lives persist after death in conditions determined by the possession or the lack of love.

The Bible is the record of God's revelation, to be used in the development of the religious life.

These are inner convictions of a continuous social movement established by Jesus Christ, which have been successively expressed in patterns acceptable to and effective in its different groups. They are the reproductive cells of the entire Christian community for they affect action and cannot be held without moral response.

VIII.

This discovery of basal attitudes and convictions through an historical understanding of the origin and purpose of doctrines leaves no mystery in the Modernists' position. Like men of the past, they are expressing and extending the permanent attitudes and convictions of Christians to the changing conditions of their own day.

The aim of the Modernist like that of all Christians is to produce in human life, as it is now being organized both socially and intellectually, attitudes and action identical with those which are genetic and permanent in the Christian movement. It is only incidentally that he attempts to prove the falsity of another's exposition of these true fundamentals. He has discovered that doctrines are only functional and interpretative of the basal faith of their origi-

nators. He would not take from any one a formula
or pattern which helps to a personal loyalty to Jesus
and a helpful way of meeting human needs. But he
knows perfectly well that some of these formulas and
patterns do not now help a large number of men to
utilize the basal Christian attitudes and convictions
in meeting needs arising from life in our modern
world. They no longer express a common experience.

But in the persistent attitudes discoverable in the
Christian group-beliefs is the permanent element of
our religion. Nothing can be fundamentally Christian that is not involved in spiritual loyalty and likeness to the religion instituted by Jesus Christ. He is
its one Foundation. The test of Christianity is active
loyalty to Christ and his message that God is fatherly
and that men, therefore, ought to be and can be brotherly. If one has only the slightest confidence in
Jesus and his message, he will not call him Lord
without striving to meet all situations by expressing
Christlike attitudes and convictions. To Jesus
hatred is sin. The mind of the Christian should
be primarily concerned with Christian activity and
not with orthodoxy or liberalism or anything that is
not moral and vitally religious. Doctrines are only
ways of aiding such conduct to intelligent expression.

Here is a real issue in the understanding of Christianity. No one can fail to see that the alternative
views of Christianity are more than the debates of
theologians. A world, a civilization, the welfare of
humanity itself are at stake. No religion can con-

tinue and be of importance that ignores the needs of souls. *Our new world cannot be made Christian by reliance upon inherited patterns, but upon Christian attitudes and convictions embodied and expressed in the Christian group's life.* As in the sixteenth century men appealed from the pope to a theory of inspiration, so Modernists appeal from a theory of inspiration to the efficiency of the principles embodied in a developing Christian religion springing from and embodyng the teaching and life of Jesus Christ. It is an issue which all who earnestly seek to serve their day will welcome. It is no time for monks or any other sort of Christians who would withdraw from this world. It is well to know just where the churches stand while the swarming millions are desperately struggling to establish justice and fraternity. If Christianity is intrinsically a system of doctrines authoritatively fixed in patterns of other times and lacking moral content, it will be abandoned. If the Christian group cannot meet to-day's needs and by its convictions inspire creative forces to make a world of justice and good will, the church will become a mere social vestige. But basal Christian convictions are a message of hope for a distracted world. They have only to be taken seriously to be a power unto salvation.

CHAPTER V.

CHRISTIANITY AS A RELIGION OF SALVATION.

THIS Christian way of life the Modernist would herald to his world. For all is not right with the world. On this men are agreed. Even those who are able to exploit and monopolize privileges have their moments of apprehension. The discontent of others seems to promise undesired change. But we are not so well agreed as to the cause of our troubles. Every man is tempted to find it in something which disturbs his own well being. Then, too, there are those who tell us that it is idle to attempt to expect any improvement, that we are so much at the mercy of economic and geographical forces that it is quite idle to plan for social betterment. That is the pessimism of naturalism.

Akin to this pessimism is that of earnest pre-millennialists who hold that the world is growing worse and more hopeless and that our only hope is the coming of Christ from Heaven to destroy it and found a new world on our earth, purified by fire. With such a view of humanity it is natural for men to look in despair upon the world from which individuals can be rescued, but which itself is doomed.

84

Yet an element of hope is involved in one of these elements of fear. The fundamental difficulty in human life is human nature, and human nature itself is not beyond hope of change. If we were mere automata, the sport of material forces, we might well despair of any better future. Development of power would mean development of misery. But we are not automata. We can do more than respond to outer influences. We have the power of initiative and choice, and, therefore, we can hope to correct the evils of the world by correcting the evils in mankind, if only we can find a way.

The Modernist is no myopic optimist. The humanity with which he undertakes to deal is the humanity turned over to him by the biologist, the psychologist and the historian, and such a humanity is something more than a doctrine. Its sin can hardly be explained by an ancient story, however true may be that story's understanding of human nature. As Christians we must again diagnose our needs and face our human tasks in full reliance upon those convictions and attitudes which lie at the center of the continuous Christian movement.

I.

Why do men need religion ? Because they distrust human power and human nature. They seek help from the superhuman power or powers upon whom they feel themselves dependent. The Christian religion is Christ's way of laying hold on God, of ordering of life which makes it possible for God to help. It is not the product of merely intellectual processes. It embodies the urge of life itself. The Christian attitude has always led to something more than itself, something mysterious and wonderful. The Christian has always believed that God gave help and saved men from sin and death. The conditions set by Christian groups for gaining this supernatural help have never been those of the intellect alone or primarily. Ritual, sacrament, prayer, penance, vows, religious training, all have aided men's souls to find God. Even orthodoxy in its more precise statements does not claim to be the aid itself, but a condition of getting aid from God. At this point Christianity has never practiced self-deception. It has never substituted faith for God.

This is the reason men pray. They are not simply expressing aspiration. They want power not their own to assist them. Sometimes such prayers are intelligent and moral, and at other times they are not, but the personal attitude of those who pray is the same; they seek help from God.

Let a man once feel his helplessness in the presence of those crises that make up his life and he will look beyond human aid. Whether he speaks of fate, or luck, or force, or God, his inner attitude is that of religion, a search for help from what is more than human.

Like all the apparatus of our human life, religious ideas and practices intended to bring help from God have sprung from and been shaped to meet our hu-

man needs. And needs are always with us. Some
of them are, one might say, atmospheric, the outgrowth of our total social life. War and pestilence,
political change and dangers, economic depression
and, when a people is prosperous, the materialism
and conflict that dog the way of wealth; these are
ever pressing in upon our spiritual life. From them
come the patterns in which we have seen our deep
Christian convictions find expression. But there are
other needs far more intimate and individual. Poverty and selfishness, sorrow and pleasure, anxiety for
our future and our loved ones, the unfaithfulness of
friends, the enmity of our associates, misunderstand-
ing in the intimacies of family and business, mis-
fortunes for which we are not responsible—all these
are a part of our common human life. Resolute and
courageous souls suffer as truly as the vacillating and
timid. And just because we are all human we turn
for aid to God. We need Him for our support and
comfort and guidance. To find Him we turn to
that religion into which we have been born or to
which we have been attracted. We pray to the God
our Christian religion gives us.

Sometimes our words are hasty and our thoughts
without help. But we cannot keep from praying.
As is our need, so is our prayer; as is our understanding, so is our confession. Religion thus becomes
a real search for some particular help. We are never
truly religious in a general way. Our religion is
most sincere when we shape our desires most by our
needs. Intelligence only makes our desires more in

accord with what we may reasonably expect. Our
growing knowledge prompts to prayer as truly as
our former ignorance. The imperfectly unified life
alone seeks to test God by demanding that He act
as if the world were different from what we know it
to be. Such religion is on the road to superstition.

All this the Modernist feels deeply. He knows the
danger of intellectual pride, of mistaking an interest
in religion for religion itself, of over-emphasizing
denials, but he also knows that his faith must not be
intellectually inert. For the sake of his religion he
attempts to analyze his needs and pray for divine aid
in the name of reality as truly as in the name of
Jesus. Now most reality is given by science. The
world of men and women has needs which must be
scientifically understood. Religious convictions must
be within the limits of such knowledge; our con-
structive patterns and organizing concepts will be
drawn from those new needs and habits and knowledge which are creative in our day.

II.

But it is not only help that men want. Across
the horizon of their future has hung like a pall the
dread of the anger of the gods or the punishment of
a supreme God. Misfortune argued guilt, and conscience confirmed the fear. The future threatened
divine retribution.

In the religion of the Jews this dread was not
superstitious but moral. The Hebrew nation had

been taught by their great prophets that their God
was not to be placated by sacrifices and that injustice
was more serious than a violation of ritual.   The
Law was the test of all mankind.   There was to be
the Judgment Day when God would punish all those
who had violated His laws or oppressed His people.

This sense of ill desert and guilt is a starting point
of the Christ's own teachings.   In the hands of later
Christian teachers it developed into forecasts of Hell
and its punishments.   But however developed, guilt
and fear of merited punishment are elements in human life that cannot be ignored.   Men remember
their mistakes and evil deeds and look with apprehension, even though it be also with bravado, at their
future.   They not only want to be helped in emer-
gencies, but they want their sins forgiven.

It is, of course, easy to discover people who
take no such serious view of life.   Some are frankly
pleasure-seekers, disregarding any law whether it be
of God, man or health, which would check their in-
dulgence.   There are others who deliberately close
their eyes to the seriousness of life and pain-giving
forces of the universe and human relations and make
optimism a religion.   But the Christian movement
has never compromised with human nature and endeavored to beguile men into easy morality.   As
Browning says,

> 'Tis the faith that launched point blank her dart
> At the head of a lie—taught original sin,
> The corruption of Man's Heart.

And it has offered men a way of salvation from that which they dreaded.

But what is salvation? An escape from being burned forever by literal flames, an entrance into an eternal vacation of song and feasting in some world in the sky? So men have believed, and some would have us still believe, for such patterns are in most Confessions. And if these pictures are treated as vigorous figures of speech intended to arouse the spiritual discontent of lives accustomed to the brutalities of the torture chambers, massacre, and remediless injustice, they are not without meaning. But they are not patterns drawn from the modern world. Our courts no longer torture, and punishment (in theory at least) is less retributive than reformatory. But we still need to be aroused to the dangers that attend sinfulness. In our rejection of medieval pictures of punishment we are in danger of indifference to outcomes. That is one reason why liberalism in theology like liberalism in politics so often lacks power. It fails to count life's fears.

But fear is more than terror. It may be a rational expectation as to outcomes. And certainly no one can seriously regard life without seeing that suffering attends wrong doing. How can we believe in a moral order if such suffering is limited to its victims? Should it not also overtake its authors? Can a man give another a contagious disease without having it himself?

This conviction that sin brings suffering can no longer be fully set forth in the terms of politics. God is more than a king or emperor. The patterns we use more naturally are derived from hygiene and medical science and embody our knowledge of life itself. To be saved is to be so transformed by new relations with spiritual forces both human and divine that past mistakes and sins have their effects offset by new life. Instead of suffering comes joy, instead of fear comes hope, instead of selfishness comes good will, instead of death comes life. Salvation is more than rescue, for rescue assures only the removal from danger; it is more than the removal of the sense of guilt and apprehension for the future. It is newness of life, a likeness to Christ which finds its expression in good will.

The way to this release from fear and the sense of guilt and to the experience of these new personal moral powers has always been held by the Christian community is found in loyalty to Jesus as the Savior. The Christian movement has never wavered at this point. Sometimes it may have too brutally portrayed the danger which lies in disobedience to cosmic will and the implacability of God's righteousness, but it has always heralded a Savior greater than that from which men need to be saved. It has preached duties with a almost relentless idealism, but it has also preached good will as a way to righteousness and the love of God as a basis of hope.

III.

How shall the Christian movement in our day organize itself so that individuals and society may sense its need and gain divine help and salvation? There are at least two sorts of answers given by those who feel the ineffectiveness of inherited doctrinal patterns. The one is that of the radical and the other that of the historically-minded.

The radical is a non-conformist who minimizes social evolution. He would say bluntly that the way in which to free humanity from its fears of divine action is to deny the legitimacy of the fear. He not only would repudiate the pattern, but he would neglect the conviction it expresses. That is one reason why the radical gets little following within the Christian movement. He is urging a reform against nature. Men know that they do need divine help because they are conscious of unworthy actions. When in the same breath they are told that religious fears are superstition and that humanity is subject to the law of causation, their anxieties may be deadened but they are not lessened. Their position is like that of the sick man who is told that it is foolish to expect suffering to come from his disease because he is subject to the law of cause and effect! It is precisely the law of cause and effect which causes anxiety.

The radical further says that we should make no effort to utilize the inheritances preserved in the attitudes and convictions of the Christian group. We are to study our needs rather than the experience of men who have carried forward the Christian movement.

The futility of such effort is apparent, for it ignores the social origin of religious formulas and the persistence of group loyalty. But it is more than futile. It serves to alienate the radical and his followers from the real world in which they live. They have forgotten folks. They have forgotten that all advances and all reforms which affect humanity must be genetic, never neglecting humanity as one factor of the problems. All reforms would be easy if it were not for folks. This holds for religion as well as for all else that is human.

The position and method of the Modernist are very different from those of the radical. He feels himself a member of a persistent group that would organize life in accordance with its spiritual inheritance. He will not overlook but would realize upon that inheritance which the group preserves. But in so doing he will discriminate between loyalty and battle-cries. Every group has its own tendencies and inhibitions quite independent from its professions. In any college, for example, "college-spirit" and customs constitute a group-control by no means always dependent upon the ideals of the institution exhibited in its catalogue. But none the less the college must develop as an educational institution and membership within it will always be determined by this general end. No one would think of joining a college faculty to transform the college into a woolen fac-

tory. So, too, is it in the Christian movement.
Loyalty to it is within the limits of its basal characteristics. In joining the movement one inherits and
is loyal to the convictions already embodied within it.
To do otherwise would be disloyal. Whether one
accepts the various patterns and methods of expressing these determining group-convictions will depend
on their efficiency in the actualities of life.

Possessed of an understanding of the Bible, a faith
in God, a discipleship of Jesus Christ, a loyalty to
as well as a knowledge of the basal, reproductive attitudes and convictions of the Christian movement of
which he is a member, the Modernist turns to his
religion as a cure for to-day's evils. In the group of
those who accept Jesus Christ as Savior is his deepest interest. He believes so heartily in the power of
God's salvation revealed by Jesus Christ and through
the Christian community that he seeks to bring it
to a world of sin. He is no theological dilettante,
no dogmatist, no radical. With God's help he means
to be a member of the body of his Lord, breaking
the bread of life to his fellows. Upon the great convictions as to the saving power of God expressed in
the various doctrinal patterns adopted by the Christian church he would build Christian living into his
own world.

IV.

As a first step to an understanding of salvation,
the Modernist comes to a more intelligent understanding of human nature and its sinfulness.

We are coming increasingly to see that the individual can be best understood by searching his history. Ancestors are keys to an understanding of disease and genius and sin alike. We know that any individual life cannot be separated from its ancestry and social environment and is, therefore, not wholly responsible for its bent and characteristics. This fact gives rise to a new sense of the complexity of any attempt to induce people to be good. We cannot detach a personality from his inheritances, and goodness must therefore always be relative. If we are to convert a person we have to convert an entire ancestry which he epitomizes in himself, as well as the influences of his social environment. What is more, we are finding that inheritances have a backward pull. As it is easier to live on an inherited income than to earn one's living, so is it easier to follow the instincts and passions which make up our inheritance from our animal and social past than to go on from them to more personal ideals and coöperation with others. Moreover, pleasure attaches to this withdrawal from moral struggle and the pursuit of outgrown goods. And pleasure always allures.

Our religion has to face these facts. As members of the Christian movement we are committed to the conviction that it is possible for an individual by God's help to be freed from the domination of his lower inheritances, that is, to be saved. When we express this conviction we shall use some formula or pattern which will not deny our scientific knowledge.

Just as our better understanding of the laws of

health have effected *materia medica* and general curative methods, so our better understanding of the problems of our human life make it possible to use our religious inheritance more intelligently as a means to salvation.

For hundreds of years following the sad days of Augustine the conception of sin was simple, expressed in the patterns of the state. God gave a commandment to the first man and woman. They disobeyed, and were put under a curse. This curse, which is that of labor, concupiscence and death, descended to their children. As men elaborated this belief it became the doctrine of original sin and total depravity which is the starting point of all orthodoxy. According to it the human race inherited the corruption and guilt of Adam, and every person ever born on the face of the earth has been born eternally lost except as God's love intervenes in choosing some for salvation.

One has only to state such a view to see how remote it is from the present day thought about wrong doing. It is not without its vigorous truth, but as a way of accounting for present day sin, such a theory is ignored by moralists and sociologists. Yet, obviously, there is suffering in the world; injustice is here; cruelty, selfishness and brutal passion are here. One gets no understanding of them by saying that they are the outcome of a sin committed by an ancestor who lived thousands of years ago, and from which there is no hope of deliverance except that of election. There is here no explanation of sin, and

there is no advantage in attempting to understand
it or to cure it.

It may be for this reason that discussion of sin, in
the theological sense of the word, is less in evidence
now than formerly. We talk more about sins, degeneracy, poverty, lust, economic oppression, war and
other concrete evils. We endeavor to understand why
some men prefer actions which benefit themselves at
the expense of others. We endeavor to protect
juvenile offenders from being regarded as criminals,
and attempt by better physical care to give them
new opportunities. We study the human condition
of a family and endeavor to prevent the marriage of
those whose children are certain to be subnormal and
criminal. We learn the technique of social progress
in order that our good will may be controlled by good
sense.

But back of wrongdoing is something more radical.
We can see that humanity is not outside of the law
of causation, and that conditions affect action. That
is to recognize God's will in human affairs. Religion
must help people under these conditions as a higher
form of life itself. Salvation results from new adjustments with God, the nature of which, thanks to
science, we are understanding better. In other words,
the Modernist looks upon sin as violation of the immanent divine will to good will and to progress towards that which is more personal; a conscious yield-
ing, because of immediate pleasure, to the backward
pull of outgrown goods; a violation of those personal
forces both of God and human society which make

progress possible. Human nature is not corrupt, but atavistic.

This is to express a basal conviction of our religious inheritance by the use of a new pattern. We are no longer thinking of man's relationship with God through the analogy of the state, but through that of life itself in which strength and development are certain when the organism and environment are in normal relations, and suffering and degeneracy attend all maladjustments.

Such a conception of sin is not abstract, but terribly real. Failure to live in right relationship with the divine and human environment on which personal life depends brings suffering. Not to practice good will is a tragic failure. Only right relations with God can save men into good will. With this sense of human need all preaching of salvation must begin.

V.

But sin is more than individual. In society, too, is the struggle against the backward pull of outgrown goods. We need religious sanction and direction not only as individuals but as inseparable members of social groups. The conceptions with which we express this relationship must be more in accordance with observed facts than any of those bequeathed by the past. Christians have always felt the dangers that lay in participating in society, but it is hard to imagine modern men as inaugurating the practices of monks and hermits. Our sense of social solidarity is too vital and too oppressive for that. The more we study our social situation, the more complex and alarming it becomes. Thoughtful Christians feel they need some more effective formula for the guidance of their religious actions than the words of the Schoolmen. We seek to organize a doctrine of the salvation which we have experienced more in accord with that recognition of justice, righteousness, good will and social coöperation in a common task which our increasing knowledge of society is compelling. We cannot justify social practices which like slavery, prostitution, war or economic selfishness treat human beings as less than personal. Ideals and practices born of a simpler social order satisfy our moral needs no more than a nomad chieftain is a satisfactory substitute for the President of the United States. Our Christian attitudes and convictions are the same in kind as those which have always characterized the Christian movement, but if a belief is really to express and justify them its formulas and patterns must be drawn from the world in which we actually live. We cannot make a dictionary of antiquities a Bible of our faith.

And, therefore, because we see that an individual becomes a person only in social relations, do we think of sin and salvation in terms which are social as well as individual. No man sins unto himself alone. Conduct is not the behavior of passive members of a social group, and the evil effects of selfishness cannot be quarantined in the individual. They live on in the group, spreading their own contagion and making life more difficult for all its members. We can think of salvation only as involving social relations, responsibilities and adjustments. We cannot imitate the church of the past in its acceptance of war and economic injustice. The entire human situation must be brought into dynamic relation with the divine Will to Love by which we are environed. The more we understand sin, the more we cry out for the presence, not only in human individuals but in society, of a God as great as our universe, as righteous as Jahweh, as loving as Jesus. Such a God and such a salvation we have revealed in Jesus Christ.

Sin is not mistaken thinking. It is actual degeneracy of personality because men hate instead of loving, are acquisitive instead of just. It cannot be overcome by good advice any more than disease can be cured by written prescriptions. There must be actual readjustment of life both individual and social. The Gospel is a power of God unto salvation, not unto merely intellectual illumination. Knowledge too often puffs up; love always builds up. Christian activity cannot be divorced from Christian teaching. What philosophy only imperfectly does, trust in God does freely. Christian faith has power and life because it brings us into proper relationship with God and man. This was the first message of the church to the ancient world. This is the appeal of supernaturalism to the common man and to the mystic. This is the appeal of Modernism as it seeks to bring men both individually and socially into intelligent, helpful relations with God. We rest our hearts on Him. The agonies and joys of human life are not beyond His fatherly care. We may not understand His ways, but with Jesus as our Master, and as partakers of the continuous influence of His church we may trust God's love. And because of our faith, we, like the countless souls who with less knowledge of His ways than ours have dared the same adventure, gain strength that otherwise we never should have felt. For God becomes a Savior when men submit their lives and their society to the spirit of Jesus through whom He is revealed. We work out our own salvation not only with fear and trembling but with hope and courage because it is this God who works with us.

CHAPTER VI.

THE GROWING FAITH IN GOD.

"I BELIEVE in God the Father Almighty, maker of heaven and earth." When one grasps the full meaning of that confession, it is as audacious as any ever uttered by human lips. It was the first conviction of Christianity to be seriously questioned. And how can we to-day hold to such a faith when we see the uniformity of nature, the suffering springing from impersonal forces and the evil issuing from men's hearts? Could a God who is both loving and omnipotent permit a world like ours to continue? So Christians of all ages have dared believe. However imperfect their philosophies, however incomplete their knowledge, they yet have trusted a God of nature whose love and salvation has been revealed in Jesus Christ. As society has grown more complicated and its needs more exigent men have turned with deeper longing to a Director of social evolution from whom can come help. An unfolding world has ever sensed a greater sinfulness and need from which have grown greater conceptions of God as an aid in bearing new burdens and facing new tasks. To carry on this process of an ever growing

102

experience of God is involved in the Modernist's
loyalty to the Christian movement.

I.

Faith in God preceded teaching. It is not the
product of speculation but of experience. The
biblical narratives record how Jahweh of the early
Hebrews was replaced by the Jahweh of the prophets,
and he in turn by the Universal Father of Jesus.
What might have been the development of this noble
unphilosophical monotheism if the Christian groups
had continued to be composed only of Jews, we can
only surmise. As it was, the change in personnel
of the early churches introduced philosophical problems of which the writers of the Bible were innocent.
The new Christian doctrine of God was not the product of philosophy, but of the attempt of men with
philosophical queries and metaphysical inheritances
to hold both to monotheism and their experience of
salvation through faith in Jesus Christ. That they
had experienced God as Savior when they believed in
Jesus as Christ they had no doubt. But how could
they believe in the Father and the Son of God and
the Holy Spirit of whom their Bible spoke without
becoming polytheists? Such a question had never
troubled the Hebrews, but was acute in the minds of
the Hellenistic Christians. The answer was reached
only after centuries of discussion. There could be
but one God-substance. Of that they were sure.
That they had met God in Jesus was equally certain.

Around these two foci the acute and creative thought of the great church Fathers swung. The debate of centuries resulted in no ultimate philosophy, but in a familiar pattern (generation) which served to express the faith of the time. The doctrine of the Trinity was thus the result of religious as well as of speculative interest. No church father or scholastic theologian ever was able to explain its intellectual content except in analogies. Yet the Trinity became a part of the inheritance of the Christian community. The constant use of a party motto expressed the unity of undoubted experiences and philosophical convictions. In it the two great streams of Hebrew and Greek monotheism joined. A metaphysical conviction was expressed in terms of biblical religion. Resolved into the experience from which it sprang, the complicated doctrine of the consubstantiability of the Son and Spirit with the Father, and of the one God-substance known in three *personæ,* expresses the profound conviction that wherever God is met He is personal. Those who had been saved by faith in Jesus Christ had been saved by God. And this conviction the Christian church still holds.

But the Trinity, like all philosophical concepts, whether they be Being or Absolute, seldom passed beyond the portals of theological thought and confessional orthodoxy. Religious trust in a God who was a present help in trouble and the basis of morality preferred to use analogies born of everyday social experience. A vernacular supplemented official language. Men thought of God as standing to them as a sovereign stood to his subjects. When once Augustine had made this the basis of faith and hope in an age of terrible social disintegration, the way of the theologian was set. He was to think of religion in terms of politics. So there came about that great theology which is a common property of all Western Christians whether they be Catholic or Protestant. God as a sovereign gave his commands to Adam. He failed to keep them and was guilty of such disloyalty as merited only punishment. Human nature became corrupt and guilty. The sovereign himself was subject to no law except that of his own righteousness, yet either because he was Love, or because he needed men to complete the perfect number of angels which had been destroyed by the fall of Satan and his followers, He wished to forgive some of these doomed rebels. Those whom he elected to salvation were to be taken into the heavenly kingdom, while all others remained in the inherited state of misery deserved by a corrupt and guilty race. To vindicate before Himself and mankind His unswerving justice in this forgiveness, God himself (in the person of the Son) made satisfaction to His injured dignity and His outraged justice by the death of the God-man on the cross. Therein men saw the reconciliation of their belief in a Sovereign's justice with His experienced love.

As nations emerged from the confusion of the feudal Empire and created monarchies, this political theology became all but self-evident. The methods of God as sovereign were described increasingly from the point of view of creative politics. Thus Englishmen who lived during the latter part of the seventeenth century and shared in the establishment of the constitutional monarchy which replaced the Stuarts, thought of God as in a way transferring his immediate control of nature to laws, something as kings transferred some of their prerogatives to Parliament. But Deism could not long endure. The pattern idea of a constitutional monarchy failed to satisfy the deepest and most penetrating religious thought. It was too novel and imperfect to be of use. The conception of God as an absolute but pardoning sovereign persisted in the evangelical theology.

The rise of democracy led men to attribute to God duties as well as rights, and after the industrial revolution and the rise of the modern *bourgeois* mind, He became increasingly thought of as the Absolute Creditor. Theology simply added the prerogatives of the capitalist to that of sovereign, and that of debtor to that of rebel. But again Christians saw God rather than men paying the debt which human sin had contracted. Theology did not so much explain as make workable and credible the Christian hope by the use of social patterns.

II.

But we have entered a world of new social customs and ideals. Men who lived in monarchies and in capitalistic states did not question the conventional patterns of theology, but those who would end monarchies, who cease to regard the present capitalistic social order as final and are instructed in scientific methods find the older patterns a hindrance rather than a help. The older conception of God, effective as it was in meeting the needs of men who lived in a certain social order, becomes increasingly inoperative with men who would change a social order. It is not that men have turned atheistic. Although many Socialists grow impatient of any idea of God as a part of the system by which capitalism has controlled the proletariat, the developing modern world has not lost its faith in God. It still looks to Him for aid and guidance. But it needs new patterns with which to coördinate its faith with its daily life, its manner of thought, its social practices and its growing knowledge of the universe. As one looks into the abysmal depths of the universe, God cannot be pictured as a sovereign in some distant heaven. As one knows more of the mystery of matter and traces the processes by which worlds are made and life evolves, He cannot be thought of as having once and for all created the world and all that is therein. Out from this insufficiency of the inherited patterns of theology to adjust our religion to our growing knowledge comes not only doubt but the threat of moral anarchy. Reality has grown so vast that the theological deliverances of a pre-scientific, monarchical age are unintelligible. Men who have grasped something of this reality seek almost pathetically some firmer basis for their moral judgments.

Our theological inheritance is not false, but for many persons, outgrown. Must they be forbidden faith in God except at the cost of their intelligence? Does knowledge stand like the angel with the flaming sword to keep out God from our modern world? It is the duty and privilege of the historical student to distinguish between formula and faith, pattern and conviction. Religious teachers again seek to re-express fundamental Christian conviction in terms which make them one with the utmost range of knowledge. There can be no no-God land between the opposing forces of naturalism and religion. Though we take the wings of the telescope and fly to the utmost reach of space, God must be there. Though we descend to the depth of atoms, there, too, He must sustain us. Though we trace the course of human evolution and social transformation, there, too, must God be found. For He is nowhere if He is not there.

To this task we are now setting ourselves with courage and with hope. Our knowledge of the universe with its laws and processes, is making us more certain that reason and purpose are immanent within its infinite activity. Matter itself has ceased to be dead, and has become vibrant with activity, instinct with order. The consensus of investigators that there is within nature a process which is evolutionary, forces us to the conviction that there must be that which is personal in that from which human personality has emerged. Our religion thus gets new support. For we can see with increasing confidence that it is a phase of life that transcends adjustment to physical and chemical environment, and seeks and gains help from fellowship with all that is personal expressed in all forces.

Metaphysics may not yet have found an ultimate formula for combining the personal elements of cosmic activity, but religion knows its God—a God who becomes more awful as knowledge becomes more vast. We may still use the language of our fathers, but we read into their patterns a meaning which transcends the figures which custom bids us use. Little by little we cease to think of the Reason and Purpose immanent in the cosmos as sovereign, and shape our ultimate conception of such limitless reality as *God*.

Nothing is more significant than the increasing use of this sacred term. In it alone we find satisfaction. It is passing from the vocabulary of philosophy into the vernacular of the heart. Kings and empires have passed but the church is praying yet. That our social experience of democracy may yet furnish some pattern idea serviceable in expressing our personal relations with this immanent God, we may well conjecture. Sovereignty is immanent in a democracy and transcendant when expressed in a government. Therein may lie a new theological pattern. But as yet the sovereignty within democracy is too unregulated and too ineffectual to express that conception of immanence to which our scientific knowledge is accustoming us. We find better patterns in science and social relations.

III.

As our conception of God has grown, changes have come in our conception of His relations to the world. The earlier stages of our religion as recorded and described in the Bible and in the faith of the Greeks were simple. We can all recall the sort of world in which we ourselves thought we lived before we knew how to extend our senses by the telescope, the microscope and other apparatus of science. Even simpler was the world of men and women who, unlike ourselves, did not find the results of science embodied in the intellectual atmosphere they breathed. Among them, as among scientists, there was seen to be the accustomed and the unaccustomed. The accustomed naturally was regarded as self-directing. The earth brought forth grass and trees, the seasons followed in regular order, stones fell to the ground, iron sank in water, and so on through the accustomed experiences of life. But the religious mind, lacking our modern knowledge of cosmic law, did not see God in these operations. He had created them and sustained them but they did not argue His continued presence. He lived in the sky. But He was not hidden from men. He had not left Himself without witness in nature; He had not abandoned His ability to do the unaccustomed. He came down from the heavens to visit men and to show His presence and His care for His people. His great power enabled Him to break across the ordinary course of events. He worked miracles. The world above nature, the sky-world, descended to the earth-world. Such revelations constituted the "supernatural."

To understand the miracle, we must come to it with the faith and limited knowledge of those men of old. It is a mistake to attempt to find the religious value of miracles by any rationalizing process. Whether there was an event or whether the miracle-story is folk-tale is of small account to the historian of a religion. The miracle-story is a form in which basal religious faith expresses itself. It is a way of picturing how God makes Himself and His personal existence known. If an axe floated it was because the spirit of Jahweh upon the prophet was able to make it float. If a great fish swallowed Jonah, it was no ordinary fish, but one prepared by Jahweh for the task. If an army was destroyed by pestilence, it was because Jahweh wished thus to deliver His people. The belief in miracles is a pre-scientific exposition of the relations of God and the world.

As men's knowledge of the uniformity of nature becomes enlarged, and they begin to speak of laws, the appeal of miracles disappears. There are seen to be other ways of saying that God is not indifferent to human needs. The fact that men increasingly think of all events as involved in the general processes of cause and effect, makes belief in miracles ineffective.

But is God any less in His world? Whoever insists upon the literalness of the miracle stories of the Bible and of the church argues that He is. He no longer walks in the cool of the day; He no longer calls upon some Abraham at the evening meal; He no longer stops the sun in order that His people may win a battle by daylight; His prophets no longer increase the supply of food and drink of widows, or raise men from the dead, or are caught up into the third heaven.

It is no wonder, therefore, that men seeing God active only or chiefly in the exception to ordinary experience, should have insisted that the supernatural (which from their point of view could be more accurately called contra-natural) is essential to religion.   Miracles are still the evidences to many earnest Christians of the very existence of God.   We do others injustice when we regard belief in the miraculous as only slavery to the letter of the Bible.   It may be that but it is also more.   It is a way of thinking of God as a very present help.   Religion itself has been identified with such considerations.   The denial of miracles seems to many tantamount to the destruction of the belief that God is actually at work in His world in other than impersonal ways; to deny that He has the power of free self-expression in ways not in accordance with laws; to feel that He has removed himself from any part in the world of affairs.   Such destruction would be in very truth to destroy the heart of religion.

The Modernist shares in this fear of banishing God from his world and of denying Him freedom.   But is belief in the existence and providence of God dependent upon the belief in super- or contra-naturalism?   Must we think of God's presence in the world only in terms used by miracle-believing minds?   There

can be no question as to the answer which will be
given by men who have been so convinced by the
evidence presented by scientific research as to feel
the supremacy of law and process in the natural
order.   To such minds, miracle in any real sense
of the word, is unthinkable.   The world-view on
which it rests has vanished.   But there is something
vastly more reassuring for faith in God in our scientific knowledge of cosmos and law, of forces of
matter and of the successive, ever more personal
stages of life.   Indeed, one might almost say that the
evidence of God's presence in our world rests upon
the precisely opposite argument from that upon which
it rested in the minds of the past.   It is the unity
of cosmic order, discoverable law and evolution
that argue the divine presence rather than some inexplicable violation of accustomed experience.   Where
God once was believed to appear occasionally, He
now is seen to be present wherever His will works
in Nature.   Science has again become the handmaid
of faith.

The Modernist assumes no *a priori* position relative to the historicity of the stories of miracles in the
biblical literature.   He recognizes their expressional
value in the religion of non-scientific minds.   He insists, however, that the records of such events should
be tested by the ordinary processes of literary and
historical criticism, and by the facts of science.   That
is to say, he asks not whether they were miracles,
but whether they actually took place.   If the evidence is strong enough to warrant belief in their

having taken place, he at once regards them as belonging to a class of phenomena which have been or will be described in some law. They are not violations of the uniformity of nature. As a religious man he does not abate one whit his belief that whether exceptional or classifiable, whether astounding or accustomed, such events are a phase of the operation of God. If there should be found only one such incident in history, as, for example, the person of Jesus Christ, the Modernist's position brings him reverently to say that therein is the unique revelation of God in accord with biological, psychological and historical processes. Indeed, the expression, revelation of God, is one with which the Modernist would express the values in the word "supernatural" when used by those who do not make the approach to reality through the methods of science, and whose thinking does not include the reign of law. Only he cannot for a moment think that God is lawless, breaking into his universe from without. He knows, too, that in some of his revelations God is more personal than in others. Just as the human personality is able to utilize forces to offset other forces, is there in the history of humanity a constant impartation of more personal to other forces. That, in fact, is the religious reading of evolution. Our heavenly Father still is working personally in His universe.

A man is to be pitied who cannot distinguish between the naturalistic, mechanistic interpretation of nature given by those who deny the existence of personality in the universe, and this position of the

Modernist who insists that the divine personality is always operating, and that evolution is an ever-increasing revelation of a Person immanent within the process itself. The Modernist is as emphatic, and one might almost say as vehement, in his denial that evolution is a Godless impersonal process, as is the most vigorous champion of super- (or contra-) naturalism. He is an outspoken and better equipped opponent of the belief that impersonal forces are sufficient to produce the human soul. An evolution in which an organism did not take in from its own environment elements of personality would be contrary to the process which science actually gives us. The evolutionary process is, so to speak, a moving picture of an infinite number of acts of God immanent in the universe and gradually imparting personality to that which, already in existence, grows more capable of personal action as its structure grows more complicated. Evolution is thus the history of an ever more complete revelation of how the infinite Person produces finite personalities.

Obviously, therefore, at this point the Modernist and the Dogmatist do not represent different religious attitudes or different religious faiths. They both believe that God reveals Himself personally through the use of impersonal means in the production of humanity. They use different scientific patterns. One says that God shaped the dust of the earth and breathed into it His spirit, and the other says that in the gradual process of the shaping up of material organisms there came a stage in which cosmic Personality—or Spirit—found new expression in some life more akin to Itself. One formula will not satisfy the intellectual methods of those who choose the other method of thought, but just as all humanity has recognized the sun as giving heat, whether it is thought of as a disk of fire or as one in a host of stars, so God is trusted and worshiped and experienced as present in His world, whether one sees the evidence of such presence in miracle stories of the pre-scientific stage or in the laws and processes of an age of science.

It is time, therefore, that we do more than distinguish between the various sorts of intellectual apparatus and patterns used in religion. Quite as imperative is it that we give full weight to the religious value of any belief by which religious attitudes and convictions are coördinated with current views of reality. But this is not the same as saying that all beliefs are equally true or in accord with reality. Farthest possible is it from saying that the champion of one intellectual world-view has the right to coerce or ridicule those who hold another. But the accuracy of beliefs will vary according to their conformity with discoverable facts. They cannot be established by votes of councils or legislatures. From this point of view the Modernist position is incalculably more tenable and defensible than that of those who demand that, in addition to a belief in the abiding and purposeful presence of a loving God in the universe, we must also believe in the literalness of the stories by which men who knew nothing of natural laws conceived that presence. Paradoxically, the miracle-story may be true and not a fact. The growing appreciation of God, the growing extension of His control which is to be seen in the history of the Hebrew religion, the philosophical conceptions of transcendency and immanence which have come from Greek and modern philosophies, the comforting and inspiring experience of God as Father due to the teaching and experience of Jesus, are not mutually exclusive. They have a unity beyond valuation for human faith. And this unity our Christian religion sets forth in its conception of God as creator, as sovereign, as Father, as Trinity and as Savior.

The God of the Modernist is not a fully understood God. Such a deity cannot be worshiped. Rationalism can never satisfy the heart of men. Mystery always lies beyond knowledge and grows into knowledge. Who knows the secrets of matter and of life? There is in us all the sense of that which is too great for our patterns to express. A God liable to cosmic bankruptcy, a God whom man must help if He be kept from failure, is no God for religious faith. He is too much like men to be worshiped. We want no God we pity, but one who, like some parabola comes out from infinity into fellowship with men, only to reach out again to infinity.

This is the God our Christian movement gives us— a God participating in human struggles but always greater than human knowledge, found by reasonable faith but not without sacred mystery. The Modernist like the believer in miracles is unwilling to stop with the ordinary, with law, with experience. He finds God personally in the entire world of facts.

And just because we see that the growing mind of men is the better able to appreciate and express a conception of God, we shrink from laying the mortmain of our own formulas and patterns, be they never so satisfactory to us, upon the future's growing knowledge and experience. So long as a pattern enables the religious life to find directive and comforting expression, so long is it sacred, and to be used. But it must not become a theological dictator of knowledge and faith. Religion must always be free to range to the very utmost reach of human thought and knowledge. To grant it any lesser privilege will be, sooner or later, to make men's growing knowledge an enemy of religion, to be checked or repudiated by those who would have faith in God. The tragedy of such antagonism can be appreciated only by those who have felt its futility.

IV.

Modernism does not stop with the assurance that the God of the Christian is the God of cosmic law and process. It trusts Him—the awful, mysterious God of abysmal space, of galaxies of stars, of ether, of evolution, of human liberty—as Father.

It is the pattern which Jesus, so full of the sense of the divine activity in sun and rain and flowers, gave to man for his comfort and his repentance. It is no term of mere good-nature. The Hebrew father was not without authority. A God who is a Father is a God who upholds the universe while He loves His children. And His love is no weak affection, but moral and self-respecting. It is God who is love, not love that is God.

This is the heart of the ever developing Christian doctrine of God. Patterns reflect men's experience but faith transcends them. When we believe in the Father we do not believe in some superman subject to the weaknesses of human wrath and feudal dignity. We think of Him as immanent reason and purpose and love in Whom we live and have our being. We carry forward the evangelical heart of Trinitarianism that God wherever met, in nature or Jesus or our own experiences, is personal. We do not grieve His Holy Spirit. We do not rest content with philosophy and doctrine. We pray to Him and trust His love which passes our knowledge. And love thus becomes a cosmic law.

To induce people to believe in such a God is to help them order their lives in accordance with His good will. Therein is salvation. To hate and injure others is to challenge God. Before Him no man can stand possessed of an unforgiving spirit. Hatred and cynicism, war and coercion must be replaced by good will or breed misery. The world as never before needs to be convinced that its evils are due to the lack of love. It needs to feel that back of history and social change is a cosmic good will abundantly able, if only men will live with it, to carry humanity forward; that good will is the only basis upon which society can rest. We cannot trust human nature that is indifferent to or hostile to the love of God any more than we can trust a denial of gravitation. As we see a good God in humanity seeking to direct its processes, setting good will as the limits within which the social life can safely proceed, we gain a basis for new moral enthusiasm and a sacrificial social-mindedness that shall replace coercion and selfishness.

It is impossible to see how the innumerable pressing needs of the world can be met by faith in any God who is thought of as less than the unknowable cosmos, or weaker than the forces of social disintegration, or distant from human hearts, or less than love. How can we come into vital fellowship with a lesser God? We need to feel the uplift of a God who is Himself sharing in men's struggle to complete a world of personal values and thus directing the divine process toward the truly personal. The Christian religion has such a God. It sees Him revealed in Jesus Christ whose life and words are the way to the Father. To approach Him is not to approach a metaphysical Absolute or a Force not ourselves making for righteousness. In such conceptions lie little power of help. Nor is it to approach a spectral personification of human values. It is to approach God as the undefined Person immanent in the universe in some such way as we finite persons are related to our bodies; upon whose good will humanity can rest in its anxieties and sorrows, its discontents and its aspirations; Who works in evolution and human history; Who is as loving and sympathetic as Jesus Christ; to Whom we can pray wtih full trust in His power and love; Who justifies our attempt to be loving; Who helps and transforms us. Faith in such a God is not the acceptance or the rejection of critical methods in the study of the Bible, imperfect theologies, the findings of scientific research. These are but the tools of men's minds as they seek better intellectual understanding. The faith of the Modernist is not a disguised interrogation. Doubts cannot be settled by doubts, but by the expansion of the life of faith itself within the angle set by our increasing knowledge. Fear is no part of such a faith. It does not view the catastrophies of nature as punishment for their victim's sins, but as unexplained operations of a cosmic Love which is constantly adding the better to the good and would have us learn that men cannot live by bread or comfort alone but by the choice of that which is personal and loving. Such faith is more than explanation—it is courage and adventurous living in a world where evils abound because the good is being supplemented by the better. It does not blink or belittle sin; it knows the bitterness of many a cross whereon men's hearts have momentarily cried that God has forsaken them. But it is a faith in a cosmic God who loves and helps and saves. The call of Modernism is a call to heroism and joy because of faith in the God who environs us. It leads men neither into pantheism, polytheism, pluralism or any other philosophy, but to a humble and trustful life of regenerating fellowship with Him Whom, through Jesus our Lord, we know not merely as maker of heaven and earth, but as the Almighty and ever present Father. It heralds no new God, but the better understood God of Jesus.

CHAPTER VII.

THE Modernist professes the Christian faith in Jesus Christ as the center of the Christian religion. Without him that religion would not have existed. Actual history enables us to see what would have been the development of the religions of the Roman Empire had there been no Jesus. Judaism would have passed through Pharisaism into Rabbinism and Talmudism; Greek philosophy would have progressed to the bounds it reached; the mystery religions, like those of Osiris and Mithra, would have temporarily expressed religious faith and would have passed away. But there would have been no Reform Judaism, no Mohammedanism, no Christianity. To-day's world with Jesus in it would never have been possible with Jesus out of it.

The approach to this epochal person can be made in two ways. We can follow up the course of Hebrew history and its growing intimacies with Hellenistic life until we reach the little group of men who believed that a carpenter of Nazareth was the one whom God had empowered by His own resident spirit to become the savior of their people. Or we can trace

123

the vast social-religious movement which we call Christianity back through the centuries until at last we can stand within this same group of believers. Both approaches are strictly historical. In both alike we must study institutions, social minds, and formulas; we must critically examine historic documents and check up our conclusions by orderly method. But each approach gives the same result. In the minds of his followers, whether they be those on the lakeside or those of the Christian centuries, the real Jesus of history has never been a mere teacher or even a prophet. He has been the unique expression of God in an individual. Nor is this all. This revelation of God in Jesus is a way to salvation for others through the influence of the personality who taught and achieved, who died and showed himself alive after his passion.

Let us reassert our conviction. Any less divine Jesus is not the real Jesus of history. His significance does not lie at points where he is like the ordinary man or even the exceptional man; it must be measured wholly in his capacity to satisfy the religious needs of men in their search for a God who is the one God of Hebrew prophet and Greek philosopher. The world is not saved by the carpenter of Nazareth, by the author of incomparably beautiful ideals, by the most representative of martyrs. *The Christian salvation centers about God in a man, not in a man made into a God.*

This is the Modernist's position. But can such a view of Jesus be substantiated? Has the Christian

church been self-deceived? Is the Christ of history
the real Jesus of Christianity? Have our critical
methods, when applied to the Bible and the Christian
religion, reduced Jesus to the companionship of
Socrates and Buddha, teachers and leaders, but not
personal revelations of God in the act of saving His
people? Is Jesus more than his teachings?

The faith of Modernism is here unshakable. By
its critical methods it has laid the doubt as to whether
Jesus actually lived. It sees in him neither the
values given him by Arius and Socinus, nor those
admitted by the purveyors of an anti-Christian naturalism. It may not use the precise vocabulary of
the Schoolmen or the Alexandrian fathers, but it
believes in the Christ those Christians interpreted
to their ages. And it will use their very terms
rather than deny their truth, for it is the successor
of those men's faith, the inheritor of their deepest
convictions. Its aim is not the production of a
philosophy or a new orthodoxy, but to make faith
in Jesus as the one in whom God revealed salvation,
possible for all men. For Jesus satisfies our supreme
moral needs.

I.

The Modernist approaches Jesus Christ through
a study of the sources at his disposal. These sources
are older than the present gospels which are beyond
all reasonable doubt the result of literary processes
extending across two or three generations of the early
Christians. Fortunately we possess complete docu-

ments from the apostolic age in the epistles of Paul, the most important of which were written within thirty years of the death of Jesus. These are the oldest written sources of the Christian movement. Mark was possibly written, and that but shortly, before the destruction of Jerusalem, but the date of the complete composition of the other two synoptic gospels no one knows with accuracy. The analysis of the synoptic gospels, however, shows that they embody material which undoubtedly came from eye witnesses. The historical student easily discovers what this material in general is by comparing Matthew, Mark and Luke, and noting first what is common to all three and then other material which is common to Matthew and Luke. The results of such comparison will not be quite identical with the original source material of the gospels, but they furnish elements which the Modernist uses for a picture of Jesus. From these earliest sources we gain no information as to Jesus prior to the appearance of John the Baptist which both Mark and Peter declare to be the beginning of the gospel. This earliest material has often been rewritten and expanded and to it much has been added, as a comparison of the gospels clearly shows. The most important of this addition to Mark and the other material common to Matthew and Luke has to do with the birth and infancy of John the Baptist and Jesus, as well as certain anecdotes of miracles and resurrection-appearances of Jesus. But these narratives do not belong to our oldest sources.

In constructing his biography of Jesus, the historian uses without hesitation this oldest material from Paul and the apostolic circle. In it he is assured is a trustworthy record of the life and teaching of Jesus. The other and presumably later material he uses or rejects according to evidence, chief of which are its agreement or non-agreement with the original sources, and the probable date of its origin.

The Jesus which emerges from this study is the Jesus of Paul and the other apostles. He is the Jesus of history. Any picture of him dependent upon the use of less critically secure material can not displace him. The Modernist prefers the Jesus of the Apostles to the Jesus of the second century literature.

If then by the use of this source material of the gospels, we place ourselves back in the original group of Christians, one fact is outstanding: they were all expecting Jesus to fulfill their expectations of a messianic salvation. They had very little else in common except what they may have inherited from their Jewish ancestry. They had no new philosophy or new religion or new ethics. There is not the slightest indication that there existed independent Christians or similar believers before Jesus had gathered this first group. They were all Jews filled with the revolutionary belief that the period of national subjection was about to close; that the God whom they served was to reëstablish them as an independent nation and lift them into supremacy over the world.

This He would do through someone He had anointed, that is to say, especially empowered by His resident Spirit. And this Coming One they believed they had found in Jesus of Nazareth. He was the one whom God had set apart and empowered by His Spirit to accomplish this wonderful revolution. He it was who was victorious over the kingdom of Satan. They apparently shared in the supernatural beliefs that find expression in the apocalyptic literature of the time. Certainly they held such beliefs later and attached them to the future activity of Jesus. But when they first gathered about Jesus it is quite as likely they were revolutionary rather than eschatological in feeling. They expected him to "restore the kingdom to Israel." Most of the teachings which Jesus gave them had to do with this hope. They were to avoid violence because God was fatherly. The kingdom of God was indeed close and at hand, but it would not come by the sword. God himself would establish it and they were to make themselves fit to join it by becoming brotherly.

Why did those early Christians come to look upon Jesus as the Christ, that is the one who was empowered by God's resident Spirit, to be this Savior? Many of them belonged to other messianic movements, one of which, that of John, Jesus himself had apparently joined, but they did not regard John as more than the herald of the coming glory. Furthermore Jesus was doing almost nothing that accorded with the current interpretations of messianic prophecy. He was not leading revolt, he was not

establishing a judgment day.   On the contrary, he
was sometimes a fugitive from ecclesiastical authority.   Yet they believed he was the Christ.   Even
when he had been crucified they could not break
from a common loyalty to him and continued to
gather in a separate group until at last they were
convinced that he had triumphed over death and
had gone to Heaven.   Thereafter their faith was
filled with hope and patience.   As before his death
they had expected Jesus to do what in accordance
with their beliefs the Messiah ought to do, so now
they expected him soon to return from Heaven and
fulfill these inherited messianic hopes of salvation.
Such faith as this could be evoked only by a personality so unique and authoritative as to make all other
definitions than that of Savior impossible.

II.

There has been no little discussion as to whether
Jesus regarded himself as a prophet or as the one
who was to establish a kingdom of God.   Some of
the answers given by various scholars, one suspects,
have been determined by dogmatic interest in Jesus'
inerrancy on the part of those who would rather
have bad exegesis than bad theology!   But the
sources show that Jesus did share in the messianic
estimate of himself; that he did think of himself
as binding the evil Prince of this age; that he did
believe he was to introduce and establish the kingdom
of God; that he did regard himself as the Son of

Man its symbol. Yet the inherited messianic hope inherited by his disciples from contemporary Judaism he attempted to correct. He was not combating Rome but the forces of evil.

Such a conviction gives significance to all his life. Clearly enough in his mind there was no separating of his official from his personal life. If he were the Christ, everything in his life was messianic. He was binding the Strong Man when he cast out demons, healed the sick, preached the gospel to the poor and gave sight to the blind. Just how far Jesus expected to have a part in some grand catastrophic act is hard to say. The gospels in their present form clearly represent the faith of the primitive church which attributes to Jesus much that was in the early Christian's own Jewish messianic expectation. Only as we arrive at the oldest documentary material embodied in our present gospels, are we on approximately certain ground. It would be pure dogmatism to start with the assertion that Jesus could not have shared in the eschatological expectations of his day, but it would be equally dogmatic to assert that he was totally indifferent to such views. The only fair method of discovering the facts in the case is that of a painstaking criticism of the documents themselves. Such an examination shows plainly that the oldest material in the synoptic gospels attribute to Jesus very few statements which partake of the apocalyptic elements so popular in the early church. Yet on the other hand it is equally plain that Jesus did not regard himself as a philosopher or social reformer. In fact, almost nothing could be farther from the picture of Jesus which lies in the oldest material at our disposal than that of a social reformer.

But while it is difficult to establish the precise degree of Jesus' participation in the current messianic expectations with which we are now so familiar, it is beyond question that he shared in the general life of his time. As Paul said, he was born under the law. As a Jew, Jesus spoke to Jews. Only after the episode of the Canaanitish woman does he seem to have gone to others. He had been sent to the lost sheep of the house of Israel. The similarities between his teachings and those of the noblest representatives of Pharasaism are marked, but he was no mere compiler of Jewish wisdom. Not only did he reject the pedantic and ascetic piety developing among his people, but he refused to think of God as merely a God of justice. He was a Father. Not punitive justice but love was the basis of Christ's ethical teaching and morality. He spoke to his fellow countrymen not in terms of nationalism, but in those of the spirit. He did not hesitate to violate the interpretation given the Old Testament by the religious leaders of his people, and he refused to combine his ideals with the Pharisees' conception of revelation. He made his teaching superior even to the Ten Commandments. If the synoptic gospels make anything clear, it is that Jesus undertook to induce people to prepare for the coming of the Kingdom by accepting his teaching as to the loving character of God and love as the condition of entrance into the Kingdom which God was to establish.

When one sees, therefore, the precise purpose that Jesus was endeavoring to accomplish, the question as to whether he held to the apocalyptic messianism becomes of secondary importance. He believed that he was the one through whom God was to introduce salvation from evil, sin and death. In adjusting himself to his world he preserved the supreme results of his nation's experience of God, and used the concepts of his day, with or without conscious accommodation. But he tried to make his followers see the difference between his ideas of the Kingdom of God and those which they themselves possessed. In this attempt he does not seem to have been successful, for current Jewish beliefs continued to be held by the members of the Christian movement. While they never regarded him as one of the rabbis, they could not grasp his own vision of the future or his profound recasting of the idea of God's reign. But one act of trust, however expressed or however obscured by their current inheritances, is central. They all believed that Jesus was empowered by God's resident spirit to accomplish their deliverance. That is the heart of the messianic definition. As compared with it, all details of hope born of inherited expectations are mere drapery. He and not any Jewish preconception or expression was central in the hearts of the first Christians. For he was Savior.

This faith in Jesus rather than the primitive messianic interpretation is the center of the Christian

religion. Each one of the elements in the conception
of messiahship was to have its own doctrinal growth,
but the central conviction that Jesus revealed God
as savior was and is to-day maintained. The conception of power given through the residence of
God's Spirit was to find new expression in the doctrines of the incarnation, the Trinity, and Christ-
ology. The conception of salvation was to pass from
miraculously established nationalism to participation
in the joys of a renewed personal life, a new social
order and the ultimate blessing of the life beyond
death. The conception of God's children was to
change from Jews to the church, the elect and those
who believe in God's fatherliness and the certain triumph of good will. But in the center of all this
development stands Jesus the Savior, the giver of
God to men, the revealer of God's way of saving men.

III.

It was the change in personnel of the original
Christian groups from Jews to Jews and Gentiles
and then to Gentiles exclusively that brought about
the first doctrinal development of Christianity as a
loyalty to Jesus the Lord and Savior. This development can be traced in the use of new and equivalent
patterns calculated to express the central place of
Jesus in the Christian salvation. Thus Paul thinks of
him not only as Christ but also as a pre-existent being
who appeared in history, the Man from Heaven. This
conception of pre-existence does not necessarily in-

volve metaphysics, but it does involve the conception
of pre-existent messiahship, which was, in other
terms, to be reëxpressed later by Origen.   All men
were regarded by the Jewish thinkers of Paul's day as
pre-existent, but Jesus pre-existed ever as the Christ.
In those of his letters in which Paul was least interested in refuting the arguments of the Judaizing
body of Christians, this superhuman position of Jesus
becomes increasingly prominent.   His work was no
after-thought of God, but it had been determined
upon before the worlds were created.

Such conceptions are not philosophical in the
Greek sense of the term, but they are methods of
making plain to minds already affected by the complicated views of the Gnostics that whatever truth
lay in their all but interminable line of aeons, was
included in the significance of Jesus as the one
through whom men were brought into reconciliation
with God.   The actual Jesus of history gave content
to the hopes which Paul had for the outcome of that
salvation which was to be accomplished by the Lord
who was the Spirit.   If the Christian had working
within him the same Spirit of God that had raised
Jesus from the dead, he might expect in his own life
a similar salvation from death.   If the Savior had
no biography, the Christian had no hope.

IV.

As the membership of the churches grew increasingly Hellenistic still other equivalents were sought

for the messianic description of Jesus' saving work.
In fact, the whole messianic scenario was in need
of reconstruction as the generations passed and no
Lord appeared from the skies.

By the second century he is said to be the incarnation of the Logos or Word. This term had already
gained currency among the philosophers as expressing the active presence of God. It was natural for
it to be used as the Hellenistic equivalent of Christ.
Thus, Jesus the Christ was described also as the
incarnate Word who had been from the beginning
with God, and who was the agent of God in creation. This, of course, is less a religious than a
metaphysical concept. Had it been substituted for
the word Christ, the idea of salvation would have
been largely lost. But the term seems not to have
had a long popularity. By the third century it has
all but been supplanted by the conception of the
Son of God, a biblical synonym of Messiah, far more
capable of theological expansion than Word. But in
the case of the Son, as of the Word, the term is one
of experience. The Son had become what Christians
were in order that they might become what he had
been; that is to say, immortal both in spirit and in
body.

Here again one must distinguish between faith
in Jesus as the one through whom God mediates
salvation and the particular formula and pattern in
which this faith was expressed. Loyalty to Jesus
as Savior was the same whether he was described
as the one to fulfill Jewish messianic hopes, or as

the incarnate Son who brought light and incorruption to human nature, or the Logos the Teacher. The church has always been convinced that his power is not due to his humanity but to the presence of God within him.

The technical controversies over the person of Christ which rocked the Christian church for a century or more raised no question as to his saving power. Athanasian and Arian, Nestorian and Eutychian all alike were agreed on this point. Their differences were those of metaphysical explanation and exposition. It was unfortunate that such differences should have all but obscured the points of identity, and lamentable that constant controversy should have diverted the Christian religion away from the moral and spiritual teachings of Jesus to the interests of the metaphysician and the lawyer. But all this does not obscure the fact that the center of the new movement was a consciousness of salvation wrought by God through Jesus Christ. Metaphysics only furnished the pattern in which men's religious needs found satisfaction. The mediator of salvation was ever more clearly not a philosophy but a person.

This concentration of religious interest upon a divine and saving personality has continued throughout the history of the church. As men's views of what salvation consisted in or implied have changed, their presentation of Jesus as Savior has also varied. Ransom to Satan, a means of satisfying divine honor, a vindication of God's justice, an example of divine love—these are but a few of the various patterns in which this pervading central thought of Jesus as the one through whom God revealed salvation has found expression. This is a supreme fact, for in it is evidence that Jesus actually is the Savior. A continuing group would not have gone on attributing to him that in which their experience showed they were deceived. The fact that men have found religious satisfaction in their loyalty to Jesus argues the sanity of their conviction that God was in him reconciling the world to Himself. That is the religious heart of the belief in his metaphysical deity. Real God has been met when men trust a real Jesus as His revealer and seek divine fellowship and salvation through him.

Such a religious conviction led to still other doctrines. The early church with its habit of thinking in terms of substance and essence found itself confronting the question as to whether the super-human elements that were found in Jesus were really of the same substance as the divine Father. The settlement of this question which found expression in a formula said to be that adopted in Nicea and known as the Nicean Creed, was not concerned with the historical Jesus of Nazareth, but with the structure of the Godhead. It is true that the religious use of the term Jesus Christ has sometimes obscured this distinction, but the Nicean Creed did not pronounce specifically on the question of the deity of the historical person, but expressed the simple belief that the eternal pre-existent Son incarnate in Jesus Christ is of the same substance of the Father, begotten not made.

It is sometimes asserted that the Nicean Creed represents that which has always been held by the church. The element of truth in such a statement is that the Nicean Creed was a way of expressing in certain terms and intellectual apparatus, a permanent conviction as to the saving revelation of God through Jesus Christ. But certainly neither the language nor the conception of "substance" found in the Nicean Creed is in the Bible or in the first Christian writers. Nor is the complicated psychology of the Creed of Chalcedon. To say, therefore, that such formulas are a sufficient epitome of the essence of Christianity is to establish tests which would exclude the apostles if not Jesus himself from the Christian religion.

But this is not to deny what is popularly known as the deity of Christ, that is to say, the revealed presence of God to be met in his life. Such a fact the Modernists as a class earnestly affirm. Nor do they deny the Nicean Creed. They regard it as historical expression of permanent convictions and loyalties. The entire history of the doctrine about Christ is included in the Modernists' faith in him. They only ask and propose to exercise the same liberty in the choice of patterns in their day as Clement of Alexandria and the members of the Council of Nicea exercised in theirs. The formulas which they use have for them the same religious function in their religious life as the Hellenistic formulas had in the life of men who were dominated by the now abandoned philosophy of substance. In function such formulas are not metaphysical but religious. The Modernist without halting to answer questions propounded by those who elevate metaphysics, psychology and church authority above religion, confesses his reverent loyalty to the basal conviction of the continuous Christian movement that Jesus is the revelation of the divine way of salvation, the Son whom to see is to see the Father.

V.

It is natural that Christians should attempt to account for this unique power of Jesus to minister like God to their religious needs. In the New Testament we have three explanations. There is the statement in all the four gospels and in Paul that his power was due to the coming upon him of the Spirit of God. This is clearly enough the natural content of the messianic conception. It is in this official sense that the term "Son of God" is used in New Testament literature, carrying forward apparently contemporary usage of the term. The Son is uniquely like the Father. Those like him are the sons or children of God.

The second explanation is that of Paul already mentioned. Jesus as Christ was the Man sent from Heaven. But this is really a variant upon the messianic conception because Paul constantly thinks of him as the Christ. His application of the term

"Lord" to Jesus perhaps carries over more of the current super-naturalism as expressed in other oriental religions, but in itself it carries no explanation of his power.

The third explanation is found in the sections prefixed in Matthew and Luke to the gospel of Mark. According to this material, the coming of the Holy Spirit was at the time of Jesus' conception. In consequence of this Jesus is said to have been born of a virgin. In these accounts, however, God is not spoken of specifically as the father of Jesus. With our present knowledge of biology and the genetic relations of the human individual before and after birth, the influence of God's spirit through the mother in the prenatal stage is not excluded. What Jesus was among men he must always have been among personalities, and his life, like all lives must have begun before birth. If he were unique as a man, he must have been unique from conception. Such an influence of the Holy Spirit upon an unborn child through the mother does not of necessity carry with it the denial of a human father, and such a view is not likely to be rejected by any believer in the influence of God on man. But it is not that of the two Infancy Sections. In them the virginity of Mary is expressly declared. The first question the Modernist as an historian raises is, therefore, one as to the literary material itself and not as to the possibility of a virgin birth. Are additions to Mark's original gospel and other source material historically trustworthy? It is necessary to emphasize this question because it is claimed that if the answer were negative doubt would be cast upon the legitimacy of Jesus. This is utterly to mistake the point at issue. The question has to do with the literary sections as wholes. Each account of the life of Jesus before his public appearance rises or falls as a whole. If it is not accepted on literary evidence, Jesus would be what Luke's gospel calls him, the son of Joseph.

Now the facts here are obvious to even a casual student of the New Testament. There is no reference to the birth of Jesus in what criticism has decided to be the earliest source material. Mark and Peter alike say that the gospel began with John the Baptist. There is no reference to the virgin birth of Jesus in Paul or in any sentence of the New Testament outside of the sections under discussion. True, Jesus is called the Son of God, but this was a synonym of Messiah and cannot be interpreted as referring to his birth. Even in Luke's gospel Mary speaks of Joseph as the father of Jesus and both she and Joseph are said not to have understood the reference of the boy Jesus to God as Father. Both genealogies of Jesus are those of Joseph. The oldest New Testament manuscript in existence (the Sinaitic Syriac Version) while containing the infancy sections declares explicitly that Joseph begat Jesus. Mary is said to have regarded Jesus as beside himself in the midst of his public work. So complete is the silence of the New Testament about the virgin birth of Jesus that even conservative theologians hold that no one of his disciples knew anything concerning it until long after his death. Then, it is conjectured, Mary told the story. But there is absolutely no evidence claimed for this. We know only that by the beginning of the second century the belief in the virgin birth of Jesus was common, not in all, but in those sections of the Christian community which finally organized the beliefs of the Christian movement.

Indelicacy attends any discussion of the biological difficulties involved in the parthogenesis of a human being. It must suffice to say that arguments from the lower animals prove too much or nothing, and that our knowledge of biological facts makes a human virgin birth as difficult of belief as our knowledge of astronomy makes it impossible for us to think that day and night existed before the sun was created. We shall leave further discussion of this matter to those who do not feel the indelicacy. It is not needed after one answers the problem of the sources. *If these are authentic we have miracle pure and simple. If they are not authentic there is no further problem to answer.*

VI.

And thus we come to the real basis of confidence in what the church calls the deity of Christ. It is the religious appeal of Jesus himself, his power to evoke religious faith. Only by attributing to him that which ordinary men do not possess can we account for his continuing influence in human life.

To make this plain is the purpose which lies beneath so much of the discussion of the past. Men have refused to believe that Jesus could have influenced them as he has unless there had been within him power which they themselves did not possess. Legend and myth have repeatedly given men divine status, and there have been plenty of demi-gods and heroes, but Christianity does not thus regard Jesus. Christians have refused to raise a man to the rank of God but they have persistently proclaimed that in and through the personality of Jesus Christ God was manifesting Himself.

With this religious trust in Jesus Christ men have comforted themselves and will continue to comfort themselves. For he functions in life as a revelation of God, not as a man who has been given apotheosis. In looking to him we find ourselves praying to the God whom we conceive to be like him. In him we feel that we can see as much of God and of His character as is possible for an individual to express. Metaphysical explanations we leave to the metaphysicians. Our faith in Jesus does not rest on the solution of the enigmas of being, or "substance," or "natures." Our starting point is the experience of God which comes when men accept Jesus as Lord. This experience has been too many million times repeated to be denied. Down through the entire history of the Christian movement men who have taken Jesus at the supreme valuation at their disposal, have found life eternal in him. We, too, believe God can save because He has saved through His revelation in Jesus.

CHAPTER VIII

JESUS AND HUMAN NEEDS

JESUS CHRIST, the Savior, rather than dogma or even the Bible, is the center of the Modernist's faith. It cannot well be otherwise. The Christian community has never been limited to the acceptance of abstract formulas. Its religion concerns more than the intellect. It is enriched by prayer and faith and the adjustment of life to ideal ends. As the Christian community throughout the centuries has faced sorrow and joy, poverty and wealth, persecution and success, social decay and growth more has been needed than truth. Men look to their religion for guidance and help. Whatever its theology the Christian movement has relied upon a God revealed as Savior in Jesus Christ.

How simple is the way to divine assistance, every Christian knows. Its center is faith in Jesus Christ and action in accordance with his life and teaching. And Jesus is not a dogma about Christ, but the historic person giving God to men.

I.

This conviction of Christians is always reasserting itself as the challenge of new needs sounds. It still dominates the Christian movement. But our

144

conception of Christ must be competent to meet the needs of our day as well as those of the past.   The Christ who satisfied the non-political, slave-holding, non-industrial, pre-scientific Christians of New Testament days too often seems only a beautiful memory in a world of machines, massed capital and labor, democracy, emancipated women, warring nations and harnessed nature.   What sort of salvation can he bring to such a world?   So long as men lived in a world refused the right of political agitation and social reconstruction, they could think of him as regent and king.   But in a world where everything is in ferment, where the very foundations of morality are being ex-examined, where the complications of social life make even the Roman Empire look simple, how shall we get aid from Christ?   The Galilean seems a strange companion for philosophers and scientists, financiers and politicians, militarists and diplomatists, purveyors of amusement and writers of books.

The fact is Jesus himself is on trial.   If there lies within the Christian movement centering about him any ability to apply its convictions regarding him to human needs, now is its opportunity.   For, outside of a narrowing group, intelligent men do not believe that God's love is limited by the practices of the feudal age, or that it needs to be justified by the sacrifices of the Pagan and Hebrew worlds. They do not think it worth while to consider whether Jesus had one nature or two, one will or two, one person or two.   They are not concerned about his being a ransom to Satan, a satisfaction to divine dignity or a substitutionary victim to divine justice. They cannot use, with any real satisfaction, the theological systems formed of the patterns drawn from politics they have outgrown and repudiated. The Christ they need cannot come to them in either the garb of a Jewish provincial or of a medieval ascetic. If he has no message capable of meeting the needs of our day he will join the company of those whom the world admires in history but ignores in life.

Loyalty to Jesus as the one competent to reveal the saving power of God whatever may be the need of humanity, is at the heart of the Christian movement. The Modernist knows no other center for his faith. He seeks only to make that loyalty a source of power. He wishes to introduce Jesus Christ to the world, believing that the world needs him and that he can help satisfy the world's needs.

But, in such presentation he would meet the modern world on its own basis. Its needs must be met by a Christ who is not an archaeological problem or a theological doctrine but a person translatable into influence.

II.

Jesus cannot help men who refuse to take his teaching seriously. It is not enough to believe something about him. Men must believe him. They must undertake to put his teachings into operation. If those teachings are practicable, they will guide men toward their desired peace and happiness. If they are not practicable, they may as well be ignored now rather than later.

The Jesus of history was not a lawgiver. He was a teacher and poet. For this reason we cannot treat his words as if they were prescriptions for our daily lives. It is true that certain persons have picked out this or that saying of his and given it literal interpretation. Some insist that he commanded immersion; others, that he taught non-resistance, poverty and celibacy, the avoidance of oaths. No one, however, so far as I know, has ever undertaken to take all his teachings in the same legal fashion. Those who have insisted on literal obedience to his commands about oaths do not take literally his command to give to him that asketh. At some point men have always seen that Jesus' ethics are more than legalistic, that his words are spirit and life.

Now the teaching of Jesus given us by a critical study of the gospels is exceedingly simple: God is love, and love is the only practicable way of life. All his teachings swing around these two foci, expanding or applying this revolutionary teaching. Men need economic goods. "Seek first brotherliness convinced of God's fatherliness," says Jesus, "and these things will be added to you." Men want to live at peace with mankind, to be reconciled with their enemies. "Love them," says Jesus, "don't fight them. Treat them as you would like to have them treat you." Men wish to be forgiven by God. "That is impossible," says Jesus, "until you forgive men the injuries they have done you." Women want personal rights. "Treat them as persons," says Jesus, "and distrust evil desire." Men want justice given them. "First," says Jesus, "give justice to others."

How dare one make such adventures as these? How can one believe that such an adventurous faith is practicable? The answer of Jesus is in effect twofold: "Good-will is practicable because God the Father has built good-will into the very structure of the universe; and the outcome of life of love can be seen in my own experience." And he died rather than distrust what he taught men to believe.

It is impossible to distinguish Jesus the person from his Cause. The two are inseparable. And for this reason the Modernist refuses to be caught in the reaction from that too speculative interest in "natures" and "will" and "persons," which would center all attention upon the message of Jesus. There is a real danger that in our zeal for the gospel that Jesus preached we neglect the gospel that Jesus lived and was. Without its biographical basis the Sermon on the Mount seems beyond any possibility of realization. But also without his teaching the personality of Jesus is a constant temptation to metaphysical discussion, whereas the real tasks of to-day are practical. We want to know how to organize our industrial and social life so that men shall not exploit one another, women shall be fully treated as persons, the production and use of wealth shall minister human welfare, and nations shall live in peace.

The Modernist believes that faith in Jesus means all this, but that such a faith does not commit one to any literal use of his words as a source of the definite technique of good will. He must trust a decision as to methods to rest on his intelligence, but if for some reason he selects mistaken methods he will not abandon good will. Not for an instant would he identify that basal attitude with any formula or program. Love is more inclusive than non-resistance or even martyrdom. Some of the specific applications of his principles which Jesus made to his own day may be impossible for men living under new conditions set by our own complicated modern life, but the Christian will not, therefore, distrust his Lord's teaching as to good will. He will honestly seek ways by which it can be constructively expressed under actual conditions. It is not good will to refuse the search for the most effective means by which it can be expressed. A parent's love for his sick child is faulty if he refuses to employ the best available cure. An unintelligent, hasty idealism has been too often a source of misery. Good will needs good social technique. We are loyal to the teaching of Jesus when in accordance with the actual possibilities of mankind we adopt even preparatory measures for socializing his spirit. And in such an endeavor to apply his teachings we not only exhibit the faith he enjoined, but meet the God he revealed.

III.

Jesus is met also in the stream of convictions, attitudes, social institutions and customs which constitute the Christian movement. Even though we hesitate to grant in full literalness the claims of certain churches, it cannot be denied that in this social institution the hopes and faith of those who first accepted Jesus as the Christ live on from age to age. We look to him, therefore, not merely across the centuries as one embodied in a literature, but also because we are members of a group that reaches across the centuries back to him and perpetuates within itself his words and influence. We feel his influence more personally than we feel that of Washington in the national life of America, or Plato in the intellectual life of the world. He is in the very environment which society constitutes. Our loyalty to the Christian community is thus a loyalty to its founder. Our every thought of God is influenced by his teaching and experience. For these have built into the structure of the very community of which we are members.

In other words, when we speak of meeting God in Jesus and of coming to God through him, we mean that we use not only the experience and the words of Jesus but also the influences born of our membership in the Christian group to help us form a conception of God and of the way to meet Him. How significant this fact is will appear if only we attempt to imagine what our conception of God would be

if our thought of Him was determined by our recol-
lection of Mohammed, or even David, and the social
unities each established.   As long as we are a part
of the ongoing Christian community we cannot separate the influence of Jesus from our faith in God.
When we say we are in fellowship with him, we
are not merely thinking of an historical character
who lived long ago, but of God as revealed in that
character.

IV.

Yet it would be a mistake to say that Jesus sur-
vives simply in literary records as the preacher of
moral ideals, religion and a supreme cause, and in a
social inheritance.   He has for us value as an historical fact.   Even more than when men saw in
him the metaphysical contact of "natures," does he
have a distinct meaning for everyone who would
take him seriously.   His entire experience furnishes
revelatory data.   He was sinless in the sense that
he met actual moral issues and always acted in the
interest of that which pertains to the common good.
In that victory is a revelation of a new morality.
His life is not a problem in the psychology of multi-
ple personalities, but a drama of human destiny.
His words about salvation are not speculative but
autobiographical; he himself is the illustration of
salvation.   Humanity with Jesus in it is not the
same as it was before his birth.   For what do the
data of his biography disclose?   Fundamentally this,

that the soul that implicitly believes in God as love, and lives perfectly that sort of life which love dominates, is saved from fear, from despair, sin, the mechanism of life, and even from death itself. He is a Savior because he was saved.

Once sharing in his own sense of God in his experience we are like him. We too shall find the Father. We are sure that reliance upon a God as good as Jesus is something more than merely subjective. It involves His real influences upon our entire being. Love becomes the condition of progress away from outgrown goods and control. We are more than conquerors, we are new creations. If the Spirit which raised Jesus Christ from the dead dwell in us, then we can hope not only for moral strength but for development into freer individuality through death itself. For salvation is not artificial or judicial. It is an advance in the total personal life made possible by a new and an advanced relationship with the personal God, the way to which is seen in the experience of Jesus. It is a still further step in human evolution which has already so largely freed personality from the control of impersonal forces through the working of a fatherly God.

V.

It is here, therefore, that the Modernist sees meaning in the resurrection of Jesus. The uncertainty which attends the historical testimony to the Virgin Birth is lacking in the case of the resurrection.

The oldest documents which we have, the letters of Paul, speak of it distinctly. It lies deep within the faith of the ancient church. One must, of course, admit the possibility, if not probability, that certain of the anecdotes that have found their way into various gospels are not strictly historical. Discrepancies between the various accounts of the resurrection appearances have been noted by all students of the gospels and the attempts to shape a unified narrative are as old as Christian literature. But the Modernist is not particularly concerned to determine to what extent all the anecdotes of the gospels are literal. He knows that some experience took place. Of this there can be no question. He is willing to wait to discover whether or not it can come within the field of what psychology explains, but he knows that even if some of these narratives be legendary they are historical expressions of the early faith that Jesus had shown himself alive after his passion. And in this faith preserved by the Christian movement he shares.

As to the precise nature of these events he does not pretend to say. Impartial criticism makes any final theory difficult. Evidently Paul did not know the nature of the resurrection-body of Christ. It is incredible that when the question as to the body of the resurrection was raised by the Corinthians, he should have turned to analogy if he possessed history. If he knew that the body of Jesus contained flesh and bones, and that he actually could eat food, it is hard to see how he could ever have said that flesh and blood were not to inherit the kingdom of God.

But this does not mean that we deny Jesus' continued personal existence beyond death. Whether his body came out of the tomb or his appearances to his disciples are explicable only by abnormal psychology, he is still living personally in whatever may be the conditions in which the dead now are.

If it is to be argued that such a position is just as truly miraculous as the belief in the emergence of the physical body from a tomb and its ascent through the air into the sky, the answer is immediate. It may be just as inexplicable, but it is not so incredible. The fact is, the more details are brought into the foreground of this resurrection faith of the disciples, the more difficult does the faith become. We can believe Paul more easily than we can believe all of the incidents given by Matthew, Luke and John. The very uncertainty and silence of the Apostle permit freedom in explanation which is estopped by the precision of the anecdotes in the three gospels. And if one is to accept any ancient fact on the basis of evidence one must cling to the evidence which seems to one to be most reliable. It is logically inconclusive to say biblical stories are true because the Bible is true. The Modernist refuses to commit himself to any such line of argument, but rejoices that the available evidence leads him to share in the deep conviction of the Christians of all the past that Jesus survived death and made himself known to his disciples. This in itself is precious beyond computation. For now we believe that the life of love though beaten down by hatred and violence, is subject neither to its origins nor to death. It is not to be expressed in the data of chemistry or of animal behavior. Since we hold to the heart of the meaning of the resurrection we refuse to have our faith in that central fact of the endless power of a Christ-like life jeopardized by doubt of statements relative to eating and drinking, traveling, wounds and disappearances. Whoever feels no difficulties in accepting such reports may well hold to them. But the faith of the Modernist in the risen Jesus does not rest upon them. It rests rather upon the trustworthy testimony of Paul, the critical recovery of the sources of the gospels, and the continued influence of the faith of the disciples embodied in the Christian movement. And with this faith he checks his grief at the death of those he loves and looks forward with a holy curiosity to his own departure. If Christ lives we shall live also.

VI.

Therefore, too, the Modernist sees meaning in the death of Jesus. Christ does not save by dying, but he died because he saved. His death is an element in the revelation of the way of salvation.

The Christian church has always found more than tragedy in the suffering and death of Christ. In the apostolic church his death was a shock to the messianic interpretation of his life, but gained evangelical meaning when coupled with the resurrection. But the two were too often divorced. As the apologetic methods of the new faith developed, the death of Christ was placed on the plane of the sacrifice of the Gentile and Jewish religions. This interpretation is on the pages of the New Testament as well as those of the Fathers. It was a pattern of undoubted help to those accustomed to see in sacrifice an element in both pagan and Jewish religions. Yet it is only a pattern. Strictly speaking Jesus was not a sacrifice. He was not offered for his friends by a priest on an altar; he was executed by his enemies upon a cross. As long, however, as the practice of sacrifice continued in the world from which the Christian group drew its members it was not necessary to do more than use it as an analogy; but that it was not central in the thought of the church is evident to any reader of the literature of the early centuries. Yet it became a part of the group-belief, to be developed far beyond an analogy in later years when the disappearance of sacrifice as a social practice led men to use biblical figures literally and build doctrines upon them.

For the first thousand years of Christian history the favorite way of expressing the meaning of the death of Christ was to declare that he had been given as a ransom to Satan in return for Satan's release of men of faith who had died before his coming. Such an interpretation seems grotesque if not immoral, but to men of the Middle Ages accustomed to seeing prisoners ransomed there was nothing impossible in the view. It was a pattern helping them explain alike his death and the salvation of the dead saints.

A new conception of the death of Christ, however, emerged under the influence of feudalism. It became the means by which God in the person of the Son is able to satisfy His own injured dignity by becoming incarnate in humanity. As the God-man, Jesus, who had no sin, was able to render satisfaction to the infinite honor of God, injured by man's disobedience. The pattern is clearly derived from feudal ideals and is altogether without biblical support. Yet it served as the basis of later views, especially in Protestantism where the death of Christ is regarded as a satisfaction of divine justice or law. The details of this view vary in different Confessions, but the underlying thought is that Jesus suffered a punishment which otherwise would have been borne by humanity itself. The source of such a pattern is clearly in the new political practices of the days in which the doctrine emerged.

The same can be said of the kindred view of modern days in which Christ is said to pay a debt owed by humanity to God, but which was beyond the power of humanity to pay.

It has sometimes been a matter of surprise that a matter so important as the death of Christ should not have acquired a dogmatic statement comparable with the person of Christ or the Trinity. The reason for this is, however, not hard to find. Within the ancient church the transformation of the meal eaten in memory of Christ into a sacrificial meal was easy. Christians like the followers of other religions ate their God. The practice grew more sacred and mysterious than any doctrine could possibly be. One might almost say that the entire church life revolved about the sacrifice by the priest of the body and blood of Christ at the altar which was then eaten and drunk by believers. The hold which this rite has on human life is undeniable. With it central the Roman church has never felt obliged to build up a dogma of atonement. It has only to celebrate the mass as a drama of faith.

On the other hand Protestant groups have increasingly made the doctrine of atonement prominent. It is not improbable that this was due to the apologetic necessity in the seventeenth century of finding some substitute for the mass. Here, as in other cases, a substitute for a Roman Catholic practice was found in a doctrine to be believed. One might almost say that what mass is to the Roman Catholic the doctrine of substitutionary atonement is to orthodoxy of the confessional type. But both alike are patterns rather than conviction and attitude. If God had not been conceived of as a king or feudal lord or as affected by the same motives as the gods of Olympus, these patterns would hardly have arisen. It follows that when the pattern in which God is conceived is changed, they like all other political or cultural corrollaries disappear, also.

But when we discern the function of these patterns which mediate Christian convictions, the death of Christ is seen to have a meaning for our modern world. The various doctrines of the atonement were intended to meet a basal difficulty in men's thought of God's foregiveness; namely, His right to forgive those who deserved punishment. How was it possible for Him to maintain His law, His justice, His dignity, if sinners were treated as if they had never sinned? Even though this difficulty disappears when one thinks of God in other than political patterns it represents permanent needs of the human heart. We cannot doubt that in some way the moral order is observed by God. The conception of what this order is has varied with the succession of social orders, but the Christian religion has always denied vacillation and unworthy motives to God. There is something heroic in the way in which men who have turned to Christ for salvation have refused to think of God as easy going. He Himself had no right to love except as His love was righteous. Such a view gives dignity to the Christian system. Even when punitive justice and wrath are portrayed with a realism shocking to our tastes, the belief that salvation never opposes righteousness is ineradicable. The moral effect of such a belief can hardly be over-estimated. If God Himself cannot indulge in lawless love how can men? And if His love leads Him to sacrifice, is it any wonder that in our day Evangelicals should have laid the foundation for so much social service?

A comparison of the doctrines of atonement will show further that the Christian church has always represented God in the person of the Son as paying

the cost of meeting the conditions of the moral order.
Humanity could not meet its obligations, but God
taking His place within humanity, by the sufferings
of the cross meets the conditions. It is a travesty of
orthodoxy to say that God has been bought off by
the death of a perfect man. What orthodoxy has always emphasized in all its successive portrayals of
the atonement is that God Himself suffered. By its
meticulous regard for trinitarianism it has rational-
ized its teaching that it was God Himself who paid
the ransom to Satan, satisfied His own dignity and
justice, paid the debt of humanity. Stripped of all
figures of speech this means that God shares in human struggles, and that man's moral progress is not
a lonesome search for an unknown good.

The Christian movement, of course, has recognized the moral influence which the courage and devotion of Jesus exerts. But its continuous conviction
is more than that. The portrayal of the death of
Christ in terms of satisfaction or substitution resolves
itself into terms of revelation. Jesus is more than a
distinguished fellow victim of injustice and bigotry.
His death is a revelation of God's participation in
human struggles, of the true perspective of evil, of
the power of the life of love, of the cost of spiritual
conquest, of the legitimacy of sacrificing secondary
goods. For if we look at the entire course of the
Christian movement, rather than at its last thousand
years, it becomes apparent that the death of Christ
cannot be separated from faith in his resurrection.
If he had not submitted to the agony born of evils

resident in our world, he could not have shown the
way to peace and purity. If he had not submitted
to death he could not have demonstrated that the life
of love is triumphant over impersonal forces and
death itself. Whether we can find a universally accepted pattern to express these facts is of small account as compared with the truth which here emerges.
*The death and resurrection of Christ help us interpret
that long evolutionary struggle from which human
life has emerged and which it carries on.* A life
which is superior to the circumstances of the impersonal world and capable of moral perfection, is
in consequence superior to death. In this sense of
embodying the end of human evolution, Jesus in his
life and death and resurrection reveals the meaning
of that process from which men have come and of
which they are a part and from which they suffer. It
is the production of individuals renewed by fellowship with God, secure in personal freedom, and
triumphing over the backward pull of inheritances
by living a life of good will in the midst of help-
giving spiritual realities.

That all progress means sacrifice men have always
known. Millions have made the supreme sacrifice of
death. But only since Jesus died as the victim of
those whom he would save, have men felt that the
law of sacrifice for ideals is a part of the divine will
that is love. And with the record of this victory we
can be steadfast, immovable, confident that a life like
his is not in vain. For we can believe that salvation
as revealed in Jesus Christ is an advanced step in

the working of God in that evolution whose history science traces, but whose end religion foresees. Now we understand why the whole creation has groaned and travailed in pain. It is giving birth to the children of God, free from the law of sin and death.

VII.

We are saved by such a hope, if only we make it motive for action. The present is evil but the future may be better. These are underlying convictions of the Christian religion. Without such hope, its frank recognition of evil and sin would make Christianity a religion of despair.

This hope is not based on merely setting up a quiescent morality after the fashion of the Buddhist. It is active, born of a belief that there are divine forces which can do more than is possible for unaided human endeavor. Human nature can be regenerated. God takes the initiative rather than simply coöperates with human effort. However difficult the logic and however outgrown the patterns with which such a conviction has been set forth, the Christian church has insisted that not only are we saved by God through faith, but that faith itself is a gift of God.

All these doctrines are eloquent as an expression of a basal attitude on the part of one who accepts Jesus as the revelation of an environing God. To such a person the struggle with evil and human weakness, the desire for freedom from the survivals of animalism which Paul called the flesh, is more than a philosophical serenity. Christians have always believed that the future was to see Jesus more influential than the present. Some day the salvation he promised will be completed; the powers of righteousness will be triumphant over evil; men will no longer be willing to benefit themselves by injuring their fellows.

This continuing inheritance of hope for the triumph of the life and ideals of Jesus has found expression in various patterns. The early Christians being Jews thought salvation consisted in the establishment of a new Jewish state in which those who were loyal to Jesus would be sitting on the throne, judging men and angels. To them the future triumph of righteousness was that of some conqueror who followed the laws of war so fearfully described by Augustine. Pictures of the coming triumph were pictures suggested by battle fields and massacres of the conquered. The picture drawn by the writer of Revelation (a writing which many churches refused to accept as canonical) portrays the expected triumph of the Christ. He was locally in the sky, whence he was to come with an archangel sounding the trumpet to summon the saints in sheol to rise to meet the coming conqueror. Then would follow a final bloody struggle with the forces of evil, the establishment of a new kingdom at Jerusalem to rule over a new and better world. From the days of the writer of Patmos to the latest expositions of Daniel and Revelation men have tried to set forth this hope with charts and diagrams. The results are themselves the best evidence of their impossibility.

That the Christians of the New Testament period expected this fearful return of Jesus is plain on almost every page of the New Testament. It could hardly be otherwise. All the details of the hope were already in their minds before they became followers of the Christ. Despite the effort made by Jesus to disabuse their minds of the hope of bloody revenge, they clung to their inheritance. After Jesus had been killed without fulfilling these desires it was natural that they should attach them to his future. Millennial exposition is demonstrably not born of the teaching of Jesus any more than was the Hebrew language. It is the way in which the Jews who instituted the first Christian group pictured salvation.

It is hard to say just how literally the early Christians took these Jewish pictures, but probably it was completely. Otherwise it would be difficult to account for some of the difficulties which arose within the early church. There is no question, however, that they expected this beatific catastrophe to occur during their life time. Paul expressly says that not all the Christians were to die. Here, of course, their mistake is obvious. Christ did not return in the sky, the archangel did not blow the trumpet, the dead did not come up from sheol to be given new bodies, there was no battle in Armageddon and there were no thrones established in Jerusalem. To anyone who knows the origin of these beliefs it is plain that their entire content is to be accepted as no more literally. So some in the early church itself saw. Already the author of the Fourth Gospel has begun to correct the messianism held by the church of his generation. To him judgment was already in the world as men showed their character by their attitudes toward Christ. Entrance into the kingdom of God was not to be by Jewish birth, but by birth of the spirit. The life of the coming age was already being lived. Christ, even when about to be crucified, had already overcome the world. His return was not to be a manifestation to all the world, but a coming with the Father into the hearts of those who kept his commandments.

Such a translation of the Jewish picture into Greek spiritual philosophy was inevitable and helpful. Men possessed of knowledge of the universe cannot take literally pictures of events taking place in the sky. They know too much about the sky. If Jesus physically ascended to some place beyond our power of sight, he must move away from the earth for thousands of years. The messianic and cosmological views of the New Testament Christians were simply a part of a Jewish inheritance. When once the Bible is properly understood there is no difficulty here. It is only when one thinks that what the Bible records is what Christianity teaches, that difficulty emerges. With the understanding of the Scriptures which is his intellectual birth right, the Modernist sees in the triumph of a returning Christ as portrayed in the patterns of the pre-christian Judaism, pictures in which a permanent attitude and conviction of Christians are expressed. For he who believes in God cannot believe that the final outcome of human experience and history is to be the triumph of that which has been once outgrown. Men who have resisted the vestiges of the animal stage, and have responded to an urge which they themselves did not originate, have moved on toward a more complete personality. As long as God operates in the human life this process must continue toward the ideals of Jesus. To no other consummation do we dare look forward. That the personality may be ennobled and developed into more complete individuality after it has been freed from animal survival by death, is a part of this hope. That is our faith in the resurrection of the body.

But there is also the nope for the Kingdom of God, a society on earth in which justice shall be mutually given and brotherliness be a measure of man's efficiency. In a world like ours such a conviction seems almost too good to be true. And it could not be true if it did not include the heart of the messianic hope that God will have a share in the building of this new social order.

Whether it be expressed in patterns of atonement or in the Jewish picture of a second coming, the Christian church has forwarded the conviction that God is working in human lives; that it is possible to discover the laws of such working; and that these laws are the way revealed in the life and teachings, death and resurrection of Jesus. We do not believe that God has made His complete contribution to human evolution. God is not emeritus. We look forward with a hope that is more than a desire to a day when, because men are embodying the attitudes and convictions of Jesus Christ in their individual and social lives, the coöperation and help of the God of law and love will make their world a social order in which love and justice will be supreme.

This is the Modernist's eschatology—an uplifting hope for a social order in which economic, political and all other institutions will embody the cosmic good will which Jesus taught and revealed; and of an advance through death of those possessed of Christlike attitudes to a complete and joyous individuality.

VIII.

Jesus cannot meet human needs without the coöperation of human life. That is the meaning of faith—not pietistic passivity or search for truth, or, much less, the mere acceptance of other men's decisions, but actual living in accordance with what Jesus supplies. The teaching of Jesus as to God and good will, the cheer of his personal example, the evidence he brings of a higher life beyond death to those who experience the saving influence of God, the divine presence in human struggles, confidence in the triumph of good will, all these lead to more than assent. They are motives, a way of life. They can be and will be expressed in living. Unlike those doctrinal patterns which constitute so large a part of Creeds and Confessions, they can be expressed in moral action. To believe them is to make them directive in all phases of our human relations. We cannot truthfully call Jesus Lord without an urge to keep his words.

It is thus Jesus meets our needs, not by miracle or philosophy, but by the appreciable revelation of the divine way for human living and human salvation. To order one's life in accordance with such a revelation is to reshape human relations and to step out into the revivifying influence of the God of the universe. That is the heart of the doctrine of justification by faith.

CHAPTER IX.

THE AFFIRMATIONS OF FAITH.

IT is poor psychology to deny that convictions underlie attitudes. Sooner or later the human heart requires the support of reason. It demands an answer to the insistent questions, What and why do I believe? Can Modernism organize any positive answers to such questions?

Not in the manner of the dogmatic mind. The Modernist movement does not seek to organize a system of theology or to draw up a confession. Modernists do not constitute a new denomination. Yet just as chemists without appeal to any authority recognize a body of facts and hypotheses which are held by those who use proper methods of chemical research, so the Modernists, because of unity of point of view and method, may be said to have reached unformulated but none the less common beliefs. Whoever attempts to epitomize this concurrence of faith will of course be giving only his own impression as to what seems to be common property of these having the same point of view and the same method of study. Such an impression, however, can be gained by a study of the literature scattered throughout all communions and countries.

Historical study gives us an understanding of the Bible and an ability to use it without hesitation as a source of religious inspiration and guidance. Similar historic methods enable us to distinguish the permanent attitudes and convictions of the Christian movement from the doctrinal patterns in which they have been expressed. We have seen how the men of the past in loyalty to their church have found new meaning in its religious convictions as they have sought to order their lives in better and more Christian fashions. We have seen how from this attempt have come the patterns and formulas with which men have unified their religion with their daily tasks. We have seen, too, how through the entire history of the Christian movement there have been deep and continuing attitudes and convictions which doctrines have expressed. We have discovered that while the making of Confessions practically was complete in the seventeenth century, men and women have carried forward the Christian movement far more extensively than the men of the seventeenth century. But we have also found that in our day there has developed a conflict between loyalty to those convictions which have been the very heart of the continuous Christian movement and the insistence upon the use of the doctrinal patterns in which they were authoritatively expressed centuries ago. On the one side are those who maintain that "the faith once given to the saints" was the doctrinal patterns; on the other, are those who see that to organize life in loyalty to the Christian movement leads the present like the past to reëxpress the inherited attitudes and convictions of the first Christian group in effective institutions and new doctrinal patterns.

I.

The religious affirmations of the Modernist are not identical with any theology. They represent an attitude rather than doctrine, they involve creative living under the inspiration of Christian connections rather than a new orthodoxy. The Modernist undertakes to project, not simply to defend permanent Christian faith. He knows that if it faces its real tasks the church cannot simply re-affirm the past. He sees something more imperative than theological regularity in the expansion of Christianity until it touches all human interest. Yet he would be consistent. If Christians find their impulses and loyalties inspired by a literal acceptance of the inherited doctrinal patterns, he would welcome their coöperation in the Christian service. It would be inconsistent for him to demand that others should accept his theology as a new orthodoxy. He must do unto others as he would have them do to him; namely, recognize the fundamental unity constituted by membership in the Christian group and devotion to the driving and reproductive convictions centering about Christ which it embodies. Let men use and permit others to use such doctrinal patterns as will make these convictions and loyalties effective in human affairs.

Earnest men are subject to temptation born of

their strength. The Modernist is no exception to this rule. If the temptation of the dogmatic mind is toward inflexible formula, that of the Modernist is toward indifference to formula. But once aware of this danger he can address himself whole-heartedly to what history and experience show to be the common divisor of Christian groups with the hope that he will thereby be of service to his day.

Tolerance is not indifference to truth that lies below doctrines. The Modernist is loyal to the Christian movement. Just as the patriot would die for his country whose laws he cannot altogether understand, so the Modernist would die for the ongoing Christian movement with its constant ministry to spiritual needs and its Christian organization of human life. He sees the need of loyalty to the Christian church, participation in its common endeavors, the organization of its members for coöperative service, the furtherance of its convictions throughout our social life. He wishes not only to make surveys, but to make converts. The Christian church is not an institution for religious research. It is the agent for ordering life among men in accordance with good will like that of Jesus Christ. However much we may need knowledge, mere intelligence is not Christian living. A man is not necessarily religious because he likes theological discussion. No man is a thorough Christian who holds himself apart from the stream of social endeavor. He should join the Christian group and share in its efforts to help men live. He cannot build himself a house by the side of the road and watch the crowd go by. That is no way to be a friend of man. Friendship means service, helpfulness, sympathy, participation in toil and weariness and anxiety, in ambitions and hopes of others. The way to get together is to work together. *We are Christians when this common effort is controlled by the attitudes and convictions which from the days of its Founder have been the heart of the continuous ongoing Christian community.*

Just because they are loyal to the convictions which have given rise to the Christian movement, Modernists cannot stop with ethics, history, science, sociology and biblical literature. They seek to come themselves and bring others into the very presence of God revealed in Jesus Christ. Only thus can they lay hold upon the God who works in the world of nature and of men. They want men to pray as well as plan, to find the way to spiritual reserves in order that they may get power to resist evil and endure success. The result of their efforts to accomplish these ends is not a philosophy but a religion enabling men and women engrossed in their daily life and social tasks to coöperate with the immanent God of love.

II.

The conviction that such a Christianity is practicable inspires every man who accepts evolution as a mode of God's activity and regards himself as not only the heir of a Christian movement but a part of a social structure which hinders even while it helps Christian ideals.

This is no new discovery. It has always been made when men have had some new and better understanding of themselves, of nature, of human needs, and of their Christian inheritance. So it was in the days of Paul, in those days of renascence when men saw that asceticism was not the Christian ideal, and in those other and more tragic days when men came to feel that humanity had rights which kings and God Himself must recognize. Christian thinkers in each epoch mediated between the continuous convictions of the church and the new spirit of progress. They used analogies drawn from the new conditions. Instead of thinking of Christ as a Jewish Messiah Paul set him forth as Lord and Spirit. Instead of thinking of salvation as made more certain by withdrawal from society, the men of the sixteenth century sought to be Christians in their daily life and in their most humble vocations. Instead of trying to persuade the revolutionists of the eighteenth century that God was an absolute monarch, Wesley taught men to think of Him as fatherly. We must follow the same method. We shall draw the analogies with which the continuous stream of Christian conviction and attitude is to be heralded from the very effort to make faith operative. If we think of God as creating man through the processes of divinely guided evolution, we shall set forth salvation as a continuation of the processes by which humanity from its first days more and more has ever appropriated God's personal influence. If we face social reconstruction we shall think of society as an accomplishment of the evolutionary process by which life builds up a more personal environment to aid it in its personal development. We shall not think of God as a monarch giving laws, or sin as a violation of statutes, or of salvation as a mere bargain between God and man. God will be ever the environing Father revealed by Jesus.

This conviction that God coöperates with efforts to reproduce the way of Jesus may find expression in new patterns drawn from democracy and the various sciences, but it may very likely be that we shall increasingly use explicitly the great Christian convictions and attitudes themselves. We shall defend those convictions by analogies and arguments capable of showing them to be consistent with the world we know, but we shall be less concerned with formulas than with the primary task of showing that the Christian life is legitimate in a world that knows nature as does ours. We shall be less concerned with patterns than with the proper way of adjusting human lives to an increasingly complicated social order, to their own capacities, to cosmic reason and purpose increasingly discoverable by the human mind and incarnate in Jesus. We may be decreasingly interested in the metaphysics of Jesus Christ, but we shall be all the more determined to show that his life and teachings reveal the divine purpose in humanity and therefore it is practicable to organize life upon his revelation of good will. And our way of expressing our basic convictions and attitudes will be more effective for our needs, for it is the outgrowth of action and social experience and is couched in the language of to-day.

In developing an intellectual apparatus for justifying the Christian life, we shall not feel the need of stressing certain doctrinal patterns which expressed the Christian convictions and attitudes of men in different circumstances and controlled by different social practices. We shall shape new patterns whenever they are needed, from life itself. But we shall not forget they are patterns.

The Modernist will cherish faith in Jesus Christ as the revealer of the saving God, but until he is convinced of the historicity of the infancy sections of Matthew and Luke, and holds different conceptions of generation from those given at present by biology, he will not base that faith upon the virgin birth as the one and only means by which God can enter into human experience.

The Modernist will not insist upon miracles, but he believes that God is active and mysteriously present in the ordered course of nature and social evolution.

Because the Modernist thinks of God as immanent within His world, he counts upon divine help in every struggle for larger freedom and justice. The death of Christ, therefore gets far richer significance for him as a revelation of such participation than is possible from analogies drawn from the sacrifices of the ancient world, the practices of feudal lords, the punishments of an absolute monarch and the demands of a severe creditor.

Because he thus sees the character of Jesus in God, and therefore believes in the possibilities of a life like that of Jesus, the Modernist will practice good will himself and urge it as the only safe and promising motive for social, economic and national life. And he will never doubt that God's good will shall some day reign on earth.

While he believes in the inevitableness of suffering from any violation of the will of God the Modernist cannot think of a literal hell with fire and burning. The ravages of disease are more terrible analogies.

Because he believes in the mystery as well as the reality of the present continued life of Christ, the Modernist will not stake this faith upon untested traditions, but will ground it on literary criticism, history and his own experience, and will therefore hope for a similar advance through death.

In fact, Modernists will very likely have no common theology whatever. They have the same attitudes and convictions as those of the historical Christian community, but they will not codify them in words of authority. They will get uniformity of point of view and expression through a common method of thought. With limitations they may prefer to use the same terms, but they are concerned primarily with Christian attitudes and convictions rather than with doctrinal patterns. They do not believe that it is possible for any body of men to express authoritatively what a group believes, so long as there is a minority of one who differs. The community of interest, the solidarity of undertaking which the Modernist knows the Christian religion involves, he will increasingly find in the activities of the Christian group to which he belongs. In this choice he will feel with certainty that he is reproducing the spirit of him who taught that his friends were those who kept his commandment to love and forgive.

III.

Although it may probably be that the day of new orthodoxies is past among those who are being trained in methods of free investigation and social organizations, new Christian service is inevitable. Modernism is not liberal dogmatism. The underlying evangelical convictions and attitudes which have been carried forward across the centuries by the succession of Christians and Christian institutions, will persevere in more active sacrificial social-mindedness. These convictions the Modernist asserts, not in the interest of theological uniformity but in the interest of a better world, of more Christlike and happier people, of institutions that will make toward justice and fraternity, and of an internationalism which will make towards peace. That such a de-theologizing of the Christian movement will produce other changes is certain. As it becomes more wide spread sectarianism will vanish and coöperation appear. There will be less of ecclesiastical chauvinism and authority, and a more intelligent attempt to put the attitudes and spirit of Jesus into the hearts of men and the operation of institutions. Christianity will grow more moral in its demands.

To what this pragmatic Christianity will tend in the development of the church as an institution remains to be seen. It is hard for me to think that we shall ever be without institutions where youth can be trained in the Christian way of life and in the defence of religion against materialism and pleasure. Nor can I imagine a world in which men and women will fail to associate themselves for worship and coöperation in the way of Christ. But whether the direction of the Christian group is to be along ecclesiastical lines, or whether it find increased expression in organizations ministering to human needs, or in both, is a matter of merely speculative interest. The community of those who hold to Christian attitudes and convictions will continue.

IV.

While by its very nature the Modernist movement will never have a creed or authoritative confession, it does have its beliefs. And these beliefs are those attitudes and convictions which gave rise to the Christian religion and have determined the development of the century long Christian movement. No formula can altogether express the depths of a man's religious faith or hope to express the general beliefs of a movement in which individuals share. Every man will shape his own credo. But since he is loyal to the on-going Christian community with its dominant convictions, a Modernist in his own words and with his own patterns can make affirmations which will not be unlike the following:

I believe in God, immanent in the forces and processes of nature, revealed in Jesus Christ and human history as Love.

I believe in Jesus Christ, who by his teaching, life, death and resurrection, revealed God as Savior.

I believe in the Holy Spirit, the God of love experienced in human life.

I believe in the Bible, when interpreted historically, as the product and the trustworthy record of the progressive revelation of God through a developing religious experience.

I believe that humanity without God is incapable of full moral life and liable to suffering because of its sin and weakness.

I believe in prayer as a means of gaining help from God in every need and in every intelligent effort to establish and give justice in human relations.

I believe in freely forgiving those who trespass against me, and in good will rather than acquisitiveness, coercion, and war as the divinely established law of human relations.

I believe in the need and the reality of God's forgiveness of sins, that is, the transformation of human lives by fellowship with God from subjection to outgrown goods to the practice of the love exemplified in Jesus Christ.

I believe in the practicability of the teaching of Jesus in social life.

I believe in the continuance of individual personality beyond death; and that the future life will be one of growth and joy in proportion to its fellowship with God and its moral likeness to Jesus Christ.

I believe in the church as the community of those who in different conditions and ages loyally further the religion of Jesus Christ.

I believe that all things work together for good to those who love God and in their lives express the sacrificial good will of Jesus Christ.

I believe in the ultimate triumph of love and justice because I believe in the God revealed in Jesus Christ.

V.

Such affirmations are more than the acceptance of biblical records, ancient facts or the successive doctrinal patterns of the Christian church. They are the substance of a faith that will move mountains. Under their control no man can deliberately seek to injure his neighbor or distrust his God. They are moral motive and direction for social action.

To trust God who is good will is to find a cure for the cynical doubt born of war and its aftermath.

To be loyal to the sinless Son of Man is to gain new confidence in the possibility of transforming human nature and society from selfishness to brotherliness.

To discover in the death of Jesus that God himself shares in sacrifice for the good of others is to gain confidence in the struggle for the rights of others.

To know that the God of law and love has made good will the only source of permanent happiness is to possess a standard of moral judgment.

To follow Jesus in international affairs is to end war.

To find God in natural law and evolution is an assurance that love is as final as any other cosmic expression of the divine will.

To embody the spirit of Jesus Christ in all action is to enjoy the peace which can come only to those who are at one with the cosmic God.

To experience the regenerating power of God is to have new hope for the ultimate completion of the human personality through death as well as life.

The final test of such generic Christianity is the ability of the Christian movement to meet human needs. And of this we have no doubt. Whoever does the will of God will know that the gospel of and about Jesus Christ is not the dream of a noble though impracticable victim of circumstance, but the revelation of the good will of the God of nature, the Father of our spirits, the Savior of His world. And through that knowledge he will gain the fruit of the Spirit—love, joy, peace, long-suffering, kindness, goodness, faithfulness, meekness, self-control.